Hans-Martin Zademach, Sebastian Hillebrand
Alternative Economies and Spaces

Hans-Martin Zademach, Sebastian Hillebrand (eds.)

Alternative Economies and Spaces

New Perspectives for a Sustainable Economy

[transcript]

Bibliographic Information published by the Deutsche Nationalbibliothek
The Deutsche Nationalbibliothek lists this publication in the Deutsche Natio-
nalbibliografie; detailed bibliographic data are available in the Internet at
http://dnb.d-nb.de

Cover concept: Kordula Röckenhaus, Bielefeld
Cover illustration: Alexandra Kaiser, Eichstätt, 2011
Printed by Majuskel Medienproduktion GmbH, Wetzlar
ISBN 978-3-8376-2498-4

Content

Acknowledgements

The volume in hand contains a collection of contributions that are concerned with alternative modes of economic and social exchange, among them alternative currency schemes, fair trade, and social enterprises. Earlier versions of these papers have been presented in the context of the study program 'Space – Society – Economy' at the Catholic University Eichstätt-Ingolstadt during the winter term 2011/12. This new program was established on the initiative of the Geography Department as a platform that aims to introduce, discuss and advance new concepts and debates at the intersections between geography, the social sciences and economics. For this purpose, each term addresses a specific topic in usually five public lectures of international guest speakers and additional work in an accompanying seminar.

It is worth noting that this study program is fully financed by tuition fees of local students; thus, first of all, we wish to thank our students for making these events possible. In this vein, we also want to thank our student assistants Julia De Gregorio and Julian Rochlitz for their excellent support in organising the series as well as valuable comments on earlier drafts of the introductory chapter. A special thanks is also due to Alexandra Kaiser for her assistance with the figures in this book and for designing the web page and further announcement materials for the study program that not least influenced the design of the cover of the book. Our team assistant Theresia

Neubauer deserves special appreciation for her great care and patience in processing all administrative tasks.

Our utmost gratitude goes, of course, to the distinguished colleagues that accepted our invitation to present and discuss selected parts of their contemporary work in course of the series; they were not deterred by the efforts to travel to wintery snowy Eichstätt, in some cases (such as in the case of Roger Lee who did the whole trip from London by train) indeed a weary journey. By dint of their insightful reflections and rich illustrations of how alternatives are performed at various scales and spaces, they offered all participants in the program, students and colleagues, a great opportunity to delve deeper into the highly relevant, challenging and exciting project to interrogate and practice alternatives in relation to and beyond economic mainstream. We hope that this volume contributes to carrying this project a little further.

Hans-Martin Zademach and Sebastian Hillebrand
Eichstätt, March 2013

Alternative Economies and Spaces: Introductory Remarks

Sebastian Hillebrand and Hans-Martin Zademach

MOTIVATION

Addressing alternatives is popular these days – most likely more than ever. This holds true for everyday life where one might feel that thinking, talking, and performing alternatives to mainstream capitalism has simply become mainstream itself, and possibly even more for academia. In this vein, also in human geography a strand of literature has developed in recent years that puts its emphasis on recognizing and explaining the large variety of alternative modes to the organisation of social and economic interaction around the globe. These alternative modes are varied; they include cooperatives and other forms of associative production, non-monetary currencies, fair or ethical trade, credit unions, local exchange and trading schemes, and the so-called social economy (Daya and Authar 2012), i.e. strategies of production, exchange, labour/compensation, finance and consumption that are in some way different from mainstream capitalist economic activity and give occasion for rethinking the economic system in itself.

Contemporary geographical research on alternative economies explores the diversity of these modes of exchange at various sites in a context-sensitive manner and exposes the dynamic relations between them at multiple scales and spaces. A particular focus is put on alternative economic means of living that are – out of necessity or sympathy – to a greater or lesser extent distant from capitalist patterns of economic behaviour. In many cases, these practices are more than marginal ideological projects: In addition to practices that render people's lives meaningful, there are practices that secure livelihoods and provide distinct solutions for those less capable to cope with the challenges of the capitalist economic system in developed and less developed societies. In this respect, the search for and enactment of alternatives to mainstream economic practices seeks to relocate power from the imperatives of capital and its imposed ideologies to individuals and collectives.

Furthermore, this research is concerned with developing an alternative conceptualisation of 'the economic' itself. That is, it not only regards the afore-mentioned variety of practices but develops a conceptualisation of the economy that is aware of the relationship between the mainstream and its alternatives and acknowledges the coexistence and interrelatedness of both 'dominant' and 'less powerful' – thus less recognised – modes of economic coordination. By means of demonstrating that alternative modes of exchange play an important role for understanding and sustaining the economic, this scholarship possesses the potential to reconfigure scholarly thinking in a broader sense and provides vital grounds to fundamentally challenge current forms of capitalism and a transition towards a more sustainable economic system.

The volume in-hand entails pieces of work associated with both lines of thinking in the discourse on alternative economies and alternative economic spaces. Evidently, this discourse has become impassioned in an unparalleled manner by the most recent global financial and economic crises. Its origins can however be traced back to times long before the first credit default swap contracts burst in Wallstreet in 2007. This chapter intends to sketch the most basic cornerstones in this field in human geography and to introduce some key notions and concepts. In doing so, the chapter seeks to establish an elementary context for addressing the variety of ways in which economic alternatives and alternative economic spaces might be approached and examined.

SETTING THE GROUND: CAPITALISM(S)

Speaking an 'alternative' economy into existence implies, first of all, that there is a mainstream economy against which the alternative is defined and qualified (Healy 2009). In large parts of the developed world, grand narratives have established a hegemonic vision of capitalism in association with progress and modernity. Put in a very simplistic manner, this vision regards neoliberal capitalism as the sole reference for any economic activity; Margaret Thatchers' well-known "There Is No Alternative" (TINA) is a particular telling manifestation of this view. By means of free trade agreements and structural adjustment programs, the capitalist ideology was spread beyond the confines of the developed world, and with the collapse of the Soviet Union and its satellites, the colonisation of formerly 'uncontrolled' spaces and societies seemed to confirm the strong narrative surrounding the expansion of neoliberal principles. This logic of market-based coordination was seen as a system that is, in its very nature, detached from society (Mingione 1991); in other words, it was claimed to establish an economic system that represents a quasi-neutral object outside the social.

In course of the worldwide expansion of the neoliberal model and the totalizing and normalizing effects ascribed to capitalism, alternative modes of economic coordination have been rendered invisible or meaningless. This can be regarded as the result of a discursive process by which capitalism has been established as the predominant set of economic and social coordination (in discursive terms 'the self'), a set that pervades all life so thoroughly that the system itself appeared to have no outside (Gibson-Graham 1996). Alternative forms of economic coordination, on the other hand, have been constructed as 'others', or as North (2007: xxii) puts it as "precapitalist holdovers or doomed utopian experiments", unable to compete with capitalism and only possible within certain forms of social organisations. The other/alternative was thus actively separated in the realm of difference while, at the same time being an integral part of (the identity of) the same/capitalism.

Important contributions to a more differentiated understanding of capitalism have been provided by studies in comparative political economy dealing foremost with the identification and differentiation of national and macro-regional models of capitalism (Rossi 2012). A particular popular approach in this field is the 'varieties of capitalism' (VoC) framework by Soskice and Hall (2001). This approach seeks to offer an institutional explanation for cross-national differences in micro-behaviour, especially that of business firms. By means of comparing capitalisms / production regimes along different institutional domains (e.g. financial systems, industrial relations, education and the training systems), this approach employs a vision of capitalist diversity opposed to the orthodox representation of a global, unitarian capitalism. Specifically, it distinguishes between two basic types of capitalisms – liberal market economies and coordinated market economies – as polar opposite ideal-types along which developed economies such as the United States, Germany, Japan, Sweden and others have been arrayed and categorized.

The argument of capitalist diversity put forward by the VoC school has been developed further within various scientific disciplines, among them political economy, new economic sociology and human geography. With regard to the debate of alternative economies and spaces, two intertwined developments may be highlighted. First, economic systems became increasingly thought beyond the territory of the nation state. As Fuller et al. (2010a: 21) put it: "[T]here has been a shift away from the fixed hierarchical thinking and territorial fetishism associated with concepts of the state, territory and geopolitics." That is, in contrast to the VoC approach's penchant for 'big picture', geographical work opts to work closer to the ground – at the subnational scale or through transnational networks (Peck and Theodore 2007).

Second, various conceptualisations have emerged that challenge the afore-mentioned idea to regard the economic as a neutral object outside the social. One key informant of this line of reasoning is Polanyi's well established concept of embeddedness. Other approaches have been predominantly influenced by neo- and postmarxist, feminist, and postcolonial approaches, which call to conceive the economy as a transformable social process and not a force of nature. In this vein, contemporary theorizations of the economic in human geography emphasise the sociocultural bases of capitalism(s) and highlight that the economic and the social are co-constitutional entities. Put in a slightly different manner: Economies / economic geographies are now widely acknowledged being not only something 'out there' subsumed under the dictate of neoliberal markets, but as socio-political constructions which are both constituting and constituted of a complex range of social relations at various scales.

KEY CONCEPTS

The just sketched differentiated and systemic micro view on capitalism can be regarded as common ground on which the key concepts applied in the contemporary discourse on alternative economies and alternative economic spaces are based upon. Quintessentially, the relationship between alternatives and mainstream is at the heart of a first important strand in the literature on alternative economies and spaces – a strand referred here to as the political economy approach. In short, this work deals with alternative economic practices *in relation to* capitalism. Parallel to this, a second strand has developed which takes into account non-capitalist practices that permeate peoples' everyday life. This perspective, labelled here as the poststructuralist account, breaks with circulating around notions and norms of capitalism; it is concerned with the recognition and enactment of diverse economies *beyond* capitalism.

The political economy approach: addressing alternative economies in relation to capitalism

The political economy perspective *relates* alternative economic practices to the conditions and contexts within economic constellations, networks, organisations or individuals. Scholars in this field take into account that many economic practices considered alternative still center on the production, exchange, and circulation of commodities: "Few are so alternative that they eschew the circulation of capital in commodity form altogether" (McCarty 2006: 808f). In fact, many alternative economic practices still focus on profit and growth, as conventional business do, and operate well within the mainstream. The key issue is thus not so much the distinction between alternative and the mainstream economic practices and spaces, but to understand how alternative and mainstream come to be defined, practiced, and reproduced in distinctive ways across space and time.

The political economy scholarship on alternative economies and spaces puts a particular focus on the deconstruction of meanings and relations of economic formations. In so doing, alternative economic practices are not merely regarded as being subject to mainstream capitalism, but as already indicated as both constituting and constituent elements of the economy and vice versa. Hence, the perspective acknowledges that the economy as an object is evident for economic efficiency and material success necessary to sustain people and society; yet, life-sustaining value is not merely esteemed in terms of economic success, but also in terms of social beliefs, objectives and values (Lee 2006). Accordingly, research on alternative economies is attentive to those involved in creating and promoting alternatives in relation to mainstream spaces of economic and political activity and the strategies that are deployed in the name of alterity (Jonas 2010).

An important analytical tool for this purpose is provided by Williams et al. (2012) who established a typology of economic practices by means of accounting for their market-orientation on the one hand, and distinguishing between monetised and non-monetised modes of exchange on the other. In this typology, the following modes were identified on the side of the non-monetised practices, arranged in the order from market towards non-market: (1) formal unpaid work in private sector; (2) formal unpaid work in public sector; (3) off-the-radar non-monetised work in organisations; (4) one-to-one non-monetised exchanges; and (5) non-exchanged labour. The spectrum of monetised practices spans, if arranged in the same logic of order, (6) formal paid jobs in the private and (7) public sector, (8) informal employment, (9) monetised community exchanges, and (10) monetised family labour.

This framework has been developed in a research project on transition economies in post-soviet Ukraine. The results of this work demonstrate that the transition to capitalism has been paralleled by development and preservation of a number of alternative and informal practices, some of them holdovers from state socialism. A large majority of the Ukraine population came to the fore as being excluded from market economic practices. It is therefore concluded that uneven development is more characterized by affluent populations that are 'work busy', participating in diverse economic practices and usually out of choice, and deprived populations more 'work deprived', conducting a narrower range of economic practices and out of necessity in the absence of alternatives (Williams et al. 2012: 229). Resolving socio-spatial inequalities can accordingly be seen as the struggle to foster engagement in the full range of economic practices that secure a livelihood rather than purely participating in the market economy.

In sum, the political economy perspective acknowledges the complex combinations and powerful interrelations of values by means of exploring the genealogies and spatial contexts of alternative economic spaces and practices. Put in discursive terms, the progressive line of thinking in the discourse on alternatives intends to transform the relation between the self as knowing and the other as object of knowledge to a view according to which both self and other constitute each other and there is no primacy for any dominant formation in a given spatial context. This reveals the possibility for various forms of economic coordination and political contestation, including the possibility to address alternative economies not only in terms of the control of economic resources, but also in terms of the control of the discourses, territories and policy paces where alternatives can find a space for themselves.

Taking diverse economies beyond capitalism –
the poststructuralist approach

Key concern of scholars following the poststructuralist performative strand of reasoning is to advance the discourse on alternative or 'diverse' economies – in this line of thinking, the expression diverse is in actual fact more common – beyond capitalist notions. For this purpose, a transformative ontology of difference is projected that aims to empower those distant others rendered invisible within the capitalist hegemony. In contrast to the "dead-end time-space of capitalism as it was usually theorized" (Gibson-Graham 2003: xxi), economic activities are regarded being located in the 'everyday economy'. That is, poststructuralist thinking takes into account and aims to unveil the multiplicity of economic relationships that are already present within the economic landscape.

Centre stage to this approach is the work of the feminist economic geographers Julie Graham and Katherine Gibson, also known as J.K. Gibson-Graham. With their work *The End of Capitalism (as we knew it)*, published 1996, they produced for many one of the most innovative and startling re-interpretations of the economy in the last decades. Two elements are particular decisive for what Gibson-Graham call a post-capitalist politics. First, they propose developing a new, more inclusive economic language:

"Our language politics is aimed at fostering conditions under which images and enactments of economic diversity (including noncapitalism) might stop circulating around capitalism, stop being evaluated with respect to capitalism, and stop being seen as deviant or exotic or eccentric departures from the norm." (Gibson-Graham 2006: 56)

Second, Gibson-Graham aim to encourage forms of subjectivity and collective agency that are open to trying new economic practices. This combination of language politics and everyday practices incites a means of imagining and enacting a politics of possibilities (Engel

2010). It constitutes space for a heterogeneity of economic practices, which do not take the logic of capital and maximizing profit for granted, and does not present them as inescapable.

An integral part of Gibson-Grahams's approach is the diverse economy framework (Table 1).[1] This framework acknowledges that many of the goods and services we rely on are obtained via exchanges in alternative and/or non-market transactions, among them local exchange trading schemes, barter and fair / ethical trade, alternative currencies, credit unions (alternative market), household flows, gift-giving, indigenous exchange, state allocations and also theft (non-

Table 1: Diverse Economies Framework

Transactions	Labour	Organisation	Property
NON-MARKET *Household flows,* *Gifts / donations,* *Indigenous exchange* *(Theft, Piracy)*	UNPAID *Volunteer,* *Housework,* *Family care,* *Self-provisioning*	NON-CAPITALIST *Worker cooperatives,* *Community* *enterprises* *(Feudal, Slave)*	OPEN ACCESS *Atmosphere,* *Open source IP,* *Outer space*
ALTERNATIVE MARKET *Local exchange* *trading systems,* *Barter, Fair trade, Al-* *ternative currencies,* *Credit unions* *(Underground market)*	ALTERNATIVE PAID *Cooperative,* *Self-employed,* *Reciprocal labour,* *In kind,* *Work for welfare*	ALTERNATIVE CAPITALIST *Environmental ethic,* *Social ethic,* *State enterprise,* *Non-profit*	ALTERNATIVE PRIVATE *State-managed assets,* *Community land* *trusts, Indigenous* *knowledge* *(Intellectual Property)*
MAINSTREAM MARKET	WAGE	CAPITALIST	PRIVATE

Sources: CEC 2001, Gibson-Graham 2006: 71, Healy 2009: 340 (modified)

---

1   Note that Gibson-Graham consider the boundaries between the various alternative modes of coordination as fluid and dynamic; a dichotomist thinking as indicated by the table might induce oversimplifying interpretations. The binaries are thus to be read rather as objects to be deconstructed.

market transactions). Similarly, the framework accounts for alternative forms of labor (e.g. volunteering), alternative and non-capitalist forms of economic organizations (worker cooperatives, non-profit organisations) and different forms of property (open source, community land trusts). According to Gibson-Graham (2008), the framing is not to be regarded as a window on a transcendent ontology. In other words, it represents simply one technology for bringing into visibility a diversity of economic activities as objects of inquiry and activism.

The diverse economies framework is regularly used for the identification of economic activities in a particular locality and for approaching the relatedness of different elements in any given practice or social location (Healy 2009). It challenges hegemonic visions of normative capitalist development and opens up the possibility for alternative localised development pathways. Gibson et al. (2010) exemplify this potential by drawing on the case of socioeconomic change in rural areas in developing countries. Most approaches addressing this change connect it to processes of unifying capitalist development for fast economic growth. If, however, the diverse economies framework is applied in cooperation with local community researchers, different insights can be gained: First, it comes to the fore that certain diverse economies are already at work at local scale that provide social and habitat maintenance, economies that could be developed further in order to achieve an increased well-being. Second, in becomes obvious that the discussion on diverse economies with local actors itself already activates participation and local experimentation and thus fosters processes of endogenous sustainable development.

As this example demonstrates, research on diverse economies is, as active intervention, not only capable of releasing positive effects of hope and possibility, but also generating alternative discourses and increasing the viability of experiments to imagine and create different futures: "What we believe, what we say, how we speak and act and see may be able to constitute new realities, new futures" (McKinnon 2010: 259). This argument builds on feminist understanding that 'the personal is political', an understanding which has fostered ways of living that have opened up a variety of politics of becoming. Feminism itself constituted a global movement that did not need to form global institutions or parties in order to be politically influential (Von Osten 2010). This suggests that against a background of an already existing vital economic and social diversity, it is possible to challenge dominant systems – an aim which is vital for people who may live in very different geographic or cultural circumstances but who share the experience of patriarchy and domination.

In sum, the poststructural scholarship focuses on the post-capitalist self as a political subject that is able to constitute new economic realities through political engagement. It intends to reveal the various forms of economic practices that already exist in the everyday economy. Instead of creating new distinctions within dominant conceptions of capitalism, the concept of diverse economies focuses on what makes our common ground for new political and economic imaginaries. By this means, it terms an epistemic break in challenging modernist conceptualisations of the economy and shows how personal efforts might play a powerful role in demonstrating the possibility of alternative economic futures.

OUTLOOK ON THE PAPERS COLLECTED IN THIS VOLUME

The five chapters in the remainder of the volume illustrate the just outlined ways to approach alternative economies and alternative economic spaces in a more comprehensive and substantially more nuanced manner. Collectively, the chapters shed light on the specific realms of inquiry into the exploration of alternative economies and spaces. In doing so, they highlight the potential of performing alternative economies in different contexts and open up a range of avenues for further empirical and conceptual work.

In detail, the next chapter by Andrew E.G. Jonas makes the case for applying a relational framework to the analysis of alternative economic spaces. Starting point of the chapter is the observation that binary thinking about alternatives has often prevailed to the detriment of knowledge of underlying social relations and territorial structures. In order to isolate some of the salient properties of alternative economic modes of exchange, Andrew Jonas suggests a set of concrete conceptual categories, namely, 'additional', 'oppositional', and 'substitute'. These conceptual categories are then applied to a case study of the British credit union movement in Hull. This case strikingly exemplifies to what extent the credit union movement in the UK is entangled in a tension between mainstream and oppositional economic and political forces around the national and local scales; in sum, a stark illustration for the point that we need a way of thinking about alternatives as evolving processes rather than fixed taxonomic categories.

In the following chapter, Peter North and Katinka Weber are concerned with alternative currencies in a political economy perspective. In a nutshell, the chapter challenges the Marxist critique of alternative economic practices being merely utopian practices by demonstrating that regional currency schemes are sustainable economic systems and valuable vehicles for strengthening local economies. This argument is developed through an in-depth analysis of the *Chiemgauer*, a rather well-established alternative currency in the south east of Bavaria. According to the results of this study, the Chiemgauer can be regarded a case in which the potential benefits of regional currencies are realized to their greatest potential. It is stressed, however, that this currency circulates in a particularly wealthy part of Germany with a distinct regional identity and strong social capital, factors that turned out being crucial for the scheme's success. Against this background and a range of further lessons to be learned from the Chiemgau (e.g. the importance of the involvement of local banks and the dedication of single persons), Peter North and Katinka Weber also elaborate on the question to what extent regional currency schemes can generally be acknowledged as factors contributing to improve local resilience.

In the next chapter, Roger Lee builds on the ideas developed by Gibson-Graham and reflects on the potential of economic difference and otherness to transform capitalist societies. At the core of this chapter is the concept of the 'ordinary economy'; this frame of the economy acknowledges that many of the social and economic relations usually termed as other or alternative represent integral parts of both our everyday social life and economic systems, i.e. it recognizes the always hybrid realities of contemporary capitalist economies. Central to this reconciliation are the complex relationships between material value and moral values (including mutuality, social justice, sustainability) that guide and shape economic activity. Applying this concept and a number of further, foremost theoretical arguments, Roger Lee develops a presumably rather realistic account of the political significance of diversity/otherness on economic change.

Subsequently, Michael Goodman and Raymond Bryant assess alternative retailing by means of a comparative investigation of Oxfam charity shops and independent worldshops (also labelled 'one-world shops') as two examples of retailers that promote the idea of more sustainable consumption. Acknowledging the aim to make a difference by helping the poor through equitable trade and access to lower cost consumption, the chapter explores the various ethical ambiguities surrounding alternative retailing – in particular, its environmental record, but also in terms of the 'spaces of intention' charity and worldshops attempt to create. According to this analysis, these ambiguous spaces of intention in Oxfam's shops, through the resale of donated goods, have resulted in the propagation of what Michael Goodman and Raymond Bryant call a 'second-hand ethics' that is unable to address the more exploitative relations under which resold clothes were originally produced. In contrast, a strict focus on fair trade at worldshops prompts a 'first-hand ethics' where the often nasty conditions of original production are indeed fully banished.

In the final chapter, Benjamin Huybrechts delivers valuable insights into the role and potential of social enterprises as agents of systemic change. As hybrid organisations at the intersection of the market and the civil society, social enterprises connect various types of stakeholders in and against the market. Using the cases of renewable energy and, again, fair trade, the chapter makes the point that social enterprises may – precisely because of their hybrid nature – contribute in a threefold manner to social and economic change: as developers of new goods and services; as pioneers in conceiving organisational models; and as creators and leaders of local and trans-local networks devoted to pursuing a transition of our economic system towards a more sustainable one. Benjamin Huybrechts however also highlights, largely in line with the previous chapters, that social enterprises cannot build and sustain systemic change alone, but are only one among a multiplicity of necessary pillars on which a socio-ecological transformation of our contemporary economic system can be conceived and built.

Taken together, the chapters make clear that addressing alternative practices of economic/social exchange and rethinking the economic is a vibrant intellectual strand in contemporary human geography. As holds true for the discipline in general terms too, the field is marked by both controversies and shared concerns. It is thus best seen as a diverse project itself, i.e. a set of approaches and schools of thought rather than a united front. As Leyshon et al. (2011) argue, precisely this lack of a canon of thought presents a massive advantage trying to come to terms with the profound challenges, both material and moral, to the functioning of the economy and thinking of alternatives. A common concern of the chapters is to exhibit the distinctive significance of space and difference in economic cultures and practices in our uneven world. Withal, they do not deny the hope that an improved knowledge about this difference and diversity provides a key to tackle the extensive economic, social and environmental dilemmas which strike at the heart of the sustainability of human life. This concern is undoubtedly worth to be sustained and carried further, not only in the academic discourse on alternative/diverse/ordinary economies, but also outside academia and the very everyday lives of all of us. There is a lot more to do – evidently, with plenty of space for economic alternatives.

Interrogating Alternative Local and Regional Economies: The British Credit Union Movement and Post-Binary Thinking

Andrew E.G. Jonas

INTRODUCTION

The inspiration for this chapter is the expanding literature in critical human geography on the production and reproduction of alternative economic spaces (see Amin et al. 2002, 2003; Lee 1999; Leyshon et al. 2003; Gibson-Graham 2006, 2008). One of the aims of this literature is to reveal the diversity of economic institutions and enterprises operating around local and regional economies (Leyshon 2005; Gibson-Graham 2011). It is encouraged by the presence and potential of alternatives to mainstream capitalist institutions and economic practices (CEC 2001; Lee and Leyshon 2003; Fuller et al. 2010b; Fickey 2011). Even as places and regions are becoming ever more drawn into global networks and circuits of capital, there is a great deal of geographical variation in terms of how people and communities engage with, experience, and reproduce economic transactions on a daily basis. As Roger Lee (2006) suggests, in a fundamental sense all economic transactions are grounded in places and regions; but especially so in the case of alternatives (Jonas 2013). The question I wish to address in this chapter is: how can we appreciate the inherent spatial diversity of economic forms in the landscape and at the same time generate new abstract categories which help to isolate some salient properties of alternative economies?

Local and regional enterprises such as complementary currencies, local exchange trading systems, credit unions, workers' cooperatives and time banks have all been identified as exemplars of the development of alternative economic spaces (Lee et al. 2004; North 2007; Seyfang 2006b; Williams et al. 2003; Daya and Authar 2012; and various contributions in Fuller et al. 2010b). Many of these enterprises are locally-operated and quasi-self-supporting economic systems which have been set up by people, communities and organisations in order to facilitate the local circulation of goods, services, currencies, and/or credit (Lee 2009). In light of the global financial crisis, the further proliferation of such alternatives offers a hopeful message about the capacity of people and communities to take control of their own economies and means of securing livelihoods (Gibson-Graham 2006; MacKinnon 2010).

Nevertheless searching questions are being asked about how we should approach and conceptualise the alterity of these putatively 'alternative' local and regional enterprises (Amin et al. 2003; Samers 2005; Healy 2009). Some scholars have pointed to an emerging rift between believers of alterity and radical sceptics (Fickey and Hanrahan forthcoming). One cause of this rift seems to have been Gibson-Graham's (1996) devastating assault on structural-Marxist methods of rational abstraction and a perceived tendency to reduce knowledge of all economic forms to pre-theorised structures of capital and class. Notwithstanding a growing sensitivity to place, difference and context (Jonas and Wood 2012), some radicals remain troubled by the ongoing disregard for Marxist theory and methods in the emerging literature around diverse economies. They have raised legitimate questions about whether a rejection of Marx's method inevitably means abandoning altogether efforts to develop concrete abstractions about the social relations underpinning alternative economic forms (Jonas 2010; North

2007). The premise of this chapter is to argue that it is possible *both* to appreciate the diversity of local economic systems *and* abstract from that diversity so as to examine the emergent properties of alternative economic spaces.

My starting point is to suggest that not all local and regional alternatives are inherently progressive in the sense that they exist and operate solely to usurp the mainstream. In fact there is nothing new in this observation. Utopian radicals such as Robert Owen and Pierre Proudhon experimented with alternative ways of combining work and leisure under cooperative industrial systems; yet despite receiving approval from Karl Marx they were later widely criticised by radical revolutionaries as bourgeois reformers (Lincoln 2003). There have been self-styled alternatives around as long as capitalism has survived; but many have since disappeared or become mainstreamed within the widening orbit of state and capital. To this day, mainstream progressive and neoliberal approaches to local and regional development operate side-by-side in the form of, respectively, 'high road' and 'low-road' labour control strategies (Gough 2012; Jonas 1996). Some radicals see benefits in the 'high road' because it privileges higher wages and labour standards than the 'low road' alternative, which is based on work intensification and harsh labour discipline. Yet these apparently divergent economic development pathways are the effects of the same sets of social relations, namely, the capital-labour relation. Perhaps the mainstream and its alternatives should likewise be examined relationally – as potentially divergent outcomes of similar sets of processes.

This chapter makes the case for applying a relational framework to the analysis of alternative economic spaces. In the earlier sections of the chapter, I show how binary thinking about alternatives has often prevailed to the detriment of knowledge of underlying social relations and territorial structures. I proceed to offer a set of concrete abstractions in order to isolate some salient properties of alternative economic forms in the landscape. These alternatives can be divided into three abstract conceptual categories, namely, 'additional', 'oppositional', and 'substitute' (Fuller and Jonas 2003). The latter sections of the chapter apply these conceptual categories to a case study of the credit union movement in the United Kingdom (UK). I argue that the alterity of the movement is not territorially fixed but has evolved, transformed and hybridised as the movement has developed and expanded across UK territory. I further demonstrate how the credit union movement is entangled in a tension between mainstream and oppositional economic and political forces operating around the national and local scales. In conclusion, I make the case for examining alterity as a relational territorial politics.

VARIEGATED CAPITALISM/DIVERSE ECONOMIES: HOW PLACE MATTERS IN CONSTRUCTING ECONOMIC ALTERNATIVES

Alternatives are flourishing in many spheres of social and economic life, ranging from the essentials, such as housing, credit, food and energy, to alternative lifestyles, music, recreation, gardening, decorating, and political activism. Whilst people have always been attracted to alternative lifestyles (if only due to an existential desire to be different), alternative economic systems tend to have an ephemeral status; they are quickly usurped by, or absorbed into, the mainstream (Schreven et al. 2008). As such, alterity must be examined as representing much more than a transient frame of mind or subjective condition. To paraphrase Samers and Pollard (2010: 49), alternatives are actively produced, reproduced and transformed in and through particular territories and are always performed and imagined collectively rather than individually. The notion that abstract knowledge of the properties of economic alternatives somehow can be detached from prior knowledge of material, social and political conditions in particular territories is a seriously flawed premise.

Attention has rightly focussed on identifying the presence of already existing alternatives within capitalism. This requires recognising the inherent diversity of economic forms in the landscape; a diversity which might not always be adequately captured by abstract categories of capital and class (Gibson-Graham 1996, 2006). Gibson-Graham has argued at length that alternative enterprises are not to be examined as pre-given social constructions; instead the categories and constructs we deploy to describe such enterprises emerge out of everyday discourses and transactions; these are the quotidian 'circuits of value' which underpin all material transactions as well as our knowledge of these transactional relations (Lee 2010b). This grounded approach opens up the possibility of identifying the properties of alternative local and regional enterprises outside of the constraints of received conceptual abstractions.

It is worth noting in passing that there are some crucial differences between Gibson-Graham's approach to economic diversity and a parallel literature which is interested in the variegated nature of capitalism (Peck and Theodore 2007). This literature itself represents a critique of mainstream work on 'varieties of capitalism' (Hall and Soskice 2001). This is the idea that the capitalism takes on specific institutional forms in different national contexts, and that identification of these 'national models' helps to explain path-dependent economic development trajectories. However, such work tends to focus on capital as an exchange relation and driven by global competition; it downplays the constitutive role of class relations, state structures and attendant territorial politics (Ward and Jonas 2004). Capitalism and its alternatives are variegated at many spatial scales. If mainstream capitalist institutions are constructed in and through particular places, regions and territories, so also are their alternatives.

Arguably the difference between Gibson-Graham's approach and that of the literature on variegated capitalism rests upon how one should conceptualise alternative social structures and their relations to territory. It does not necessarily follow that we should abandon *all* attempts at abstraction since abstractions are themselves contingent upon knowledge of historical-geographical contexts (see Cox 2012). Take, for example, Gibson-Graham's approach to class relations. She reformulates class from a high-level abstraction into a concrete concept, i.e.

into a subjective and transformative force of change which emerged from the actions of human subjects who shape their own economic destinies in particular places and regions. In this respect, the abstract category class captures a relational process of becoming rather than representing a fixed category totally devoid of territorial meaning and context (Gibson-Graham et al. 2001).

This is not inconsistent with the Marxist method of abstraction insofar as Marx was interested in understanding commodities, including labour power, not as fixed 'things' and 'objects', but rather as concrete abstractions whose properties are contingent upon their relations to other social entities (Marx 1976). The properties of wage labour cannot be isolated simply by observing it at one moment in time at the point of exchange; instead its properties arise out its relationship to capital and the overall process of production, circulation and consumption (Marx 1977). Moreover, commodity relations take on different concrete forms throughout the process of production; likewise their properties change as these relations interact and combine with other social processes and, crucially, with territory too. The challenge of concrete abstraction is to isolate the emergent properties of, say, labour power from the diversity of forms of labour occurring throughout the process of production. By abstracting from the spatial variety of labour relations, we can say something quite profound about the underlying 'structural coherence' of capitalism, class relations and territory (Harvey 1982).

To summarise, approaching alterity is not just about appreciating geographical variation and contingency within capitalism. It involves generating abstractions from detailed studies of the performance of diverse economic transactions occurring around specific places and regions. Alternative local economies cannot be pre-allocated to fixed conceptual categories; rather the concrete abstractions we use to describe their properties arise from knowledge of the social, economic and political conditions surrounding the performance of alternatives. The alterity of 'alternative' economies is itself inherently diverse, context-dependent and place specific; it is a contingent social condition whose properties arise relationally out from interactions with other (e.g. mainstream capitalist and state) processes, relations and territories.

POST-BINARY THINKING: SEEING ALTERNATIVE ECONOMIC SPACES RELATIONALLY

Notwithstanding the above remarks, work around alternative economic spaces has been quite conducive to binary thinking at the expense of relational analysis and concrete abstraction; this may be due to its fixed positioning with respect to the economic mainstream (Jonas 2010). Binary thinking about alterity is manifested by a preference for taxonomies and dualisms, such as alternative/mainstream, regulated/unregulated, formal/informal, global/local, state/market, capitalist/non-capitalist, economic/political, and so forth. The concern here is that one does not know whether these categories are designed to capture starkly opposed social forces and relations (e.g. alternative versus mainstream, local versus global, state versus market) or instead alternative economic practices which are in the process of transforming from one condition to the other (i.e. *from* alternative *to* mainstream, *from* local *to* global, *from* market *to* state, etc.). What we need is a way of thinking about alternatives as evolving processes rather than fixed taxonomic categories.

Whilst we can recognise the inherent diversity of alternative economic forms, more could be said about the territorial politics of alterity. Some alternatives are variations within existing capitalist enterprise (i.e. 'alternative capitalist' institutions). Others can conceivably be studied as operating outside mainstream circuits of capital and only later become absorbed into, or co-opted by, the mainstream. Yet others operate in such a fashion as to preserve their identity and autonomy (e.g. from the state); these, in turn, actively seek to challenge the mainstream. In each of these cases, we need to show how the category of alterity is not fixed in time and space but rather is always in motion. Alternative economies always evolve territorially, relationally and politically or, as Lionais (2010) suggests, alternative social enterprises actively embed their unique social and political values in specific institutions, laws, rules, places and regions.

A further consideration is whether the language of territory lends to the analysis of alternatives a closed discourse – that of fixed hierarchies – rather than an open and empowering language – one of flows, relations and political possibilities. It has been suggested that rigid binary thinking about scale and territory forecloses an appreciation of economic difference (Gibson-Graham 2002). For these reasons, some human geographers want to abandon rigid categories of territory and scale, replacing these with a more open language of site, relations, networks and flows (Marston et al. 2005). Yet I want to argue that in developing concrete abstractions about alternatives it might be premature to abandon altogether concepts of scale and territory (Jonas 2006). We require a language of territory and scale if only to demonstrate how 'local' alternatives are able to proliferate relationally throughout a wider territory such as the national state.

In examining alternatives, such as local currencies, North (2010) draws a useful distinction between 'strong localisation' and 'weak localisation', showing that what matters is not whether the local represents a pre-given territorial scale but rather how it enables stronger connections to be made across territory, thereby allowing alternatives to proliferate. The essence of this relational approach to territory and alternatives can be captured by the following quote, which appeared on the website for the Lewes Pound, a complementary currency based in the town of Lewes in the County of Sussex in England:

"Some ... imagine that the aim of economic localisation is complete self-sufficiency at the village level. In fact, localisation does not mean everything being produced locally, nor does it mean an end to trade. It simply means creating a better balance between local, regional, national and international markets ... Localisation is not about isolating communities from other cultures, but about creating a new, sustainable and equitable basis on which they can interact" (Norberg-Hodge and Mayo 1996: 2-3).

In other words, understanding how they relate to territory and scale is the key to unlocking the properties of alternative economies. These properties could range from self-sufficiency, at one end of the spectrum, to sustainability, at the other. Such an insight, in turn, shows the potential for developing a set of concrete abstractions which are sensitive the territorial politics of alterity.

ABSTRACTING FROM THE DIVERSITY OF ALTERNATIVE ECONOMIC SPACES

I want to begin this task by reflecting upon a selection of short quotes taken from interviews with local users of a credit union in the UK. One of my students, Rebecca Meritt, wrote her undergraduate dissertation on the credit union movement in Hull, an industrial city in the north east of England (Meritt 2010). When we discussed her conceptual approach, I suggested that she asked local users of the credit union in what respects credit unions in Hull operated as 'alternative' economic spaces. Part of the context for this line of enquiry relates to the fact that credit unions in the UK are increasingly been seen as viable savings and borrowing alternatives to mainstream financial institutions, such as banks and building societies. Amongst the various responses Rebecca obtained from her informants, three stood out because they capture the different ways in which people think about credit unions as alternative institutions. In the following extracted quotes, I have provided fictional names for the respondents in brackets (all quotes from Meritt 2010).

- Response 1 ('Mel'): "To me the credit union is not part of [mainstream] banking; it's unique, it's down there on its own and it's not part of the banking system".
- Response 2 ('Rachel'): "So yeah [the credit union] has changed my life, I have got savings now and I can say that is how I want to spend that or I can earmark it for certain things".

• Response 3 ('Stan'): "I think I see [credit unions] as helping the people that the banks can't help; I think that's their main function ... To me the whole idea of credit union is to help poor people ... It's everybody's really but particularly the poor people's ... I would always want credit unions to help people at the bottom of the pile particularly as well as everybody else".

Each of these quotes represents a different response to the question "what is alternative about credit unions in Hull?" and each says something distinctive about how one might want to think about credit unions as alternatives. Respondent 1 ('Mel') separates credit unions from the wider financial system; she sees them as offering something very different to mainstream banks. For her, it is the very localness and spatial proximity of her credit union, which makes it an alternative to the mainstream banking system. Respondent 2 ('Rachel') focuses much more on how the credit union has transformed her own life. By providing an alternative to debt, the credit union has helped her to pull through in difficult times, changing her life in the process. Response 3 ('Stan') also has a different view about credit unions as alternatives. He focuses on how credit unions are regarded as marginal institutions used mainly by those financially excluded from mainstream banks. As such they operate in a particular niche as institutions of last resort where the wider financial system has failed.

These are three quite distinct ways of thinking about and representing credit unions as alternative economic spaces in the current context of the UK. It is important to add a cautionary note, however. Those thinking about alternative institutions in these terms might be misguided and indeed, to some extent, could be wrong. For example, Stan evidently has an idealist view of banks as institutions potentially able to 'help' poor people but clearly failing in this mission. Yet the fact that Stan is not able to see that banks exist primarily to make a profit does not mean he is wrong about credit unions serving as alternatives to banks. Rachel, on the other hand, is focussed on how credit unions serve individual needs. In doing so, she overlooks how credit unions operate as collective enterprises; they would not function without collectively pooling the resources of savers and redistributing those resources in the form of interest or loans. In other words, the transformational role of credit unions depends on how they operate as a collective rather than whether they address the needs of an individual. Finally, Mel speaks eloquently about the intimacy of the credit union in terms of its relationship to the people and community it serves. So for her the 'local' is what makes credit unions alternative. However, local credit unions are part of a much wider movement and, as I will argue below, in the UK they still depend on national (and international) support for long-term financial and social sustainability.

Of course, there might be other ways of representing credit unions as alternatives. But these stories are salient because they speak to how the properties of such alternatives can be understood. In each case, it is helpful to approach credit unions as alternatives by thinking about them territorially (e.g. in terms of the geographic communities they serve) *and* relationally (e.g. how the wider development context extends out from the local to the national and international scales).

Duncan Fuller and I have divided alternatives into three conceptual categories, namely, 'alternative-additional', 'alternative-oppositional' and 'alternative-substitute' (Fuller and Jonas 2003). Each of these categories captures different senses in which enterprises like credit unions operate as alternatives; differences which are in many respects captured by the three interview quotes from the credit union respondents above. In Table 1, I have tried to isolate some of the most important properties of each of these categories. These properties relate to their constituent modes of exchange, the form of labour, the measure of value, the politics of distribution, and territorial identity.

Let me say a few more things about this. Firstly, the properties of 'additional' alternative institutions are primarily determined by the principle that they offer additional choices alongside mainstream capitalist enterprises. Many credit unions fall into this category because they are consumer collectives which operate under different sets of rules from those of banks and building societies yet still rely on the

Table 1: Key properties of different categories of alternative enterprises

	Alternative enterprise		
	ADDITIONAL	OPPOSITIONAL	SUBSTITUTE
Mode of exchange	Market Interest-bearing Complementary	Reciprocal Social credit Communitarian	Survival Gift Sharing
Form of labour	Wage Alternative wage	Non-wage Redistributive	Cooperative Socially necessary
Measure of value	Price of labour Exchange value	Labour time Use value	Needs driven Alternative value
Politics of distribution	Competitive Liberal	Anti-capitalist Populist	Self-sufficient Utopian/Anarchist
Territorial identity	Local-global	Anti-global	Local or regional

Source: author's compilation

mainstream financial system for access to interest, funding and regulation. Likewise many complementary currencies would fall into this category.

Secondly, alternative 'oppositional' institutions are usually set up in order to challenge if not usurp mainstream institutions. They tend to embody radically different (i.e. non-complementary) modes of exchange, organisational structures, mechanisms of distributing income and territorial identities to those of the capitalist mainstream. A key property of oppositional alternatives is whether they measure and perform labour time in a non-exploitative fashion such that there is some sort of equivalence in the quality and quantity of labour. A useful example of this type of institution might be time banking (Seyfang 2010).

Finally, alternative 'substitute' enterprises are economic institutions of last resort. People reliant upon such institutions might not consciously be involved in developing alternatives. Rather these sorts of institutions are needs-driven and motivated by a desire to survive, get by, or be self-sufficient. Many utopian communities and other small-scale autonomous economic enterprises have been founded with a view to becoming self-sufficient if not alternative *per se* and yet tend to have an ephemeral existence.

In the remainder of the chapter, I want to develop this analysis a bit further by showing how alternative enterprises can transform their alterity in relation to the changing landscape of territorial politics. My example is the British credit union movement and draws upon some work I did with Duncan Fuller a few years ago (Fuller and Jonas 2002, 2003) but tries to bring the story up-to-date with respect to recent regulatory and financial trends in the UK. The British credit union movement represents of good case of binary thinking insofar as a distinction is sometimes drawn between, on the one hand, credit unions embodying an 'old' model of local, small-scale and grant-dependent enterprises and, on the other, those representing a 'new' model of self-sustaining, large-scale and financially secure co-operatives. However, this binary does not explain the processes underpinning the transformation of local credit unions into different categories of alternative enterprise. I want to argue that nationally and locally credit unions are being repositioned as alternative 'additional' enterprises operating alongside, and competing with, mainstream institutions such as banks and building societies. This political repositioning actively disrupts the binary distinction between 'old' and 'new' credit union models.

THE UK CREDIT UNION MOVEMENT AS A RELATIONAL TERRITORIAL POLITICS

Whilst credit unions are well-established savings and borrowing institutions in countries like the Ireland, Australia and USA, in the UK they have remained for the most part small-scale enterprises which until recently have had little national visibility in debates about financial reform (Berthoud and Hinton 1989). The earliest community credit unions in the UK were set up in the 1960s and were associated with an influx of immigrants from countries where credit unions were more established. Many of these early community credit unions were run by local church groups and volunteers operating in the major cities like London, Birmingham, Manchester, Liverpool, and Glasgow. They tended to base their common bond around residents of low-income housing estates. The movement subsequently spread to other parts of Britain but retained a strong base in the poorer parts of major cities.

Community credit unions have generally performed well in providing low-income individuals and communities with access to credit and savings opportunities (McArthur et al. 1993). Such credit unions have been regarded as acceptable low-cost credit alternatives to payday loans, loan sharks, and other costly sources of local credit. Recognising their growing presence in British society, in 1979 the Credit Union Act was passed, enabling some local volunteer-run community credit unions to be transformed into co-operatives run on a more professional basis under the aegis of the Registry of Friendly Societies. At this stage, credit unions were very much seen as alternative 'substitute' enterprises, offering savings and credit as a last resort in communities lacking access to mainstream banking facilities.

Although the British credit union movement has often suffered from a low profile compared to its counterparts in many other countries, there has been considerable growth in the overall membership of UK credit unions in recent years, albeit this has been associated with some contraction in the number of active (i.e. reporting) credit unions. The World Council of Credit Unions reported 573 credit unions active in Great Britain in 2004 and a total of 392,438 members (WOCCU 2004). In 2009, the Financial Services Authority reported 505 active credit unions (i.e. those fulfilling FSA reporting requirements) operating throughout Great Britain (including England, Scotland and Wales) with total assets of GBP £674 million and 818,403 members (Financial Services Authority 2010) Much of this growth has been in response to the widespread closure of local branches of national banks and building societies following a wave of financial deregulation in the 1980s and early 1990s (see Leyshon and Thrift 1997). Under the New Labour government (1997-2010), the UK state used organisations like credit unions to tackle social and financial exclusion in Britain's major cities. This led to further reforms in the regulatory framework for credit unions in the 1990s, and the development of closer links between credit unions and the financial mainstream (Fuller and Jonas 2002).

In 2002, the regulation of credit unions was transferred from the Registry of Friendly Societies to the Financial Services Authority (FSA). In addition, the UK government set up a Credit Union Taskforce charged with resourcing local credit unions. It was felt that a combination of stronger national regulation and increased local authority funding could underpin the national development of the credit union movement. At this juncture, two models vied for status in the emerging landscape of credit union development in the UK (Table 2).

Table 2: Characteristics of 'old' and 'new' credit union models in the UK

	'OLD' MODEL	'NEW' MODEL
Common Bond	Community-defined within a geographic area	Work and live: not tied to a specific place
Membership	Mainly low income residents	Mixed: employees and all residents
Transactions	Save and borrow only	Savings, loans, credit, insurance, shares
Enterprise structure	Volunteer member operated	Professional cooperatives
State support	Grant-dependent	Self-funded
Spatial scope	Residential estates and city wards	City-wide and regional
Regulatory authority	Registry of Friendly Societies	Financial Services Authority
Organisational philosophy	Serving the poor and financially excluded	Financially sustainable and socially inclusive
Form of alterity	Alternative substitute	Alternative additional

Source: author's compilation

On the one hand, the 'old' model was based on the community common bond and embodied a longstanding "commitment to people and place" (Conaty and Mayo 1997). On the other, the 'new' model championed credit unions as industrial cooperatives or what became known as work-live credit unions. Advocates of the 'new' model spoke of the need for the commercial viability and social inclusiveness of industrial credit unions even if this came at the expense of a "commitment to people and place". In many respects, the further development of the movement involved a stark choice between these two 'alternative' models. To put this differently, the territorial politics of alterity within the movement was shifting such that the one model was now regarded as 'oppositional' to the other.

In the wake of the financial crisis of 2007-08, growing public mistrust of mainstream banking institutions, and the election of a national Coalition government (Conservative and Liberal-Democrat), attention has once again focused on how the legislation governing UK credit unions can be reformed. In a debate in the House of Lords on reforms to financial regulation in the UK in April 2008, the former Archbishop of Canterbury (and member of the District of Canterbury Credit Union), Rowan Williams, argued the case for credit unions as follows:

"The encouragement of locally based, entirely trustworthy, user-friendly, educationally sensitive and confidence-building methods of managing debt should be among government's highest priorities in combating ... poverty ... It is much to be hoped that fresh legislation will bring increased flexibility by, for example, enabling credit unions to work with corporate members – small family businesses, religious groups active in community work, local co-operative networks and so on – and giving the option to members of paying interest on continuing savings retained in the credit union, rather than receiving a dividend .... Furthermore, a broadening of the definition of a common bond area to enable the services of a credit union to be shared across different localities would help these organisations to move more effectively into neighbourhoods where there is no accessible credit. All these new liberties might make the credit union movement in due course as significant a presence in our credit economy as it is elsewhere" (www.publications.parliament.uk/pa/ld200708/ldhansrd/text/80425-0003.htm [May 2008]).

Subsequently introduced by UK Parliament, reforms have allowed credit unions to draw their membership from a much larger common bond area, which can include up to two million people. Whilst newly-registered credit unions still have to define a common bond area, this is no longer directly tied to particular places, organisations, or groups (e.g. a trades union). Credit unions can also offer interest payments for savers at rates that compete with banks and building societies, prompting the following headline in a well-known British tabloid newspaper: Greedy banks beware: Credit unions are a fairer alternative (Mirror, 11 January 2012).

The UK government sees credit unions not only as offering an additional choice to mainstream banks but also a more acceptable source of credit for those on low incomes as compared to the lending practices of payday lenders and loan sharks, which are increasingly seen as hyper-exploitative (Jones 2012). Further reforms introduced in 2012 include more rigorous reporting of credit union activities and the splitting of the FSA into two regulatory bodies, the Prudential Regulation Authority (PRA) and the Financial Conduct Authority (FCA). In the future, UK credit unions will be regulated by both of these new organisations.

Many of these national regulatory developments seek to steer the credit union movement towards a more sustainable, financially secure and socially inclusive 'new' development model rather than an 'old' one based upon a "commitment to people and place". However, the evolving story is much more complicated than suggested by the 'old/new' model binary because in the process the nature of credit-union alterity is itself changing. This change creates ongoing dilemmas and tensions within the movement insofar as many credit unions remain viable and credible only insofar as they can be seen to operate as institutions of last resort serving the financially excluded. Even at a very early stage in the reforms, the National Association of Credit Union

Workers (NACUW) had expressed the concern the social basis of the movement was being undermined by attempts to transform community credit unions into mainstream financial institutions (NACUW 1999). Activists within the movement therefore have been keen to reinforce a sense of local commitment, emphasising that credit unions should continue to serve financially excluded communities.

Such arguments resonate with the view that credit unions and other co-operative enterprises are being repositioned as part of the UK Coalition Government's 'New Localism' agenda. According to Featherstone et al. (2012) this agenda marks a more aggressive 'roll-back' neoliberalism. In a climate of fiscal austerity and drastic cuts in local authority funding, many credit unions are no longer in a position to focus solely on serving the financially excluded. Most community credit unions remain very small in size, have failed to generate sufficient income or surpluses to achieve financial self-sufficiency and stability, and are staffed by overworked, stressed and ageing volunteers. Many can only ever hope to serve a fraction of their potential common bond membership. Such credit unions have experienced difficulties in developing into sustainable alternative sources of credit and finance for *all* potential members and are close to insolvency. However, other credit unions have chosen to follow the national trend and seek a more commercial outlook. In doing so, these credit unions are being forced to reposition themselves both as 'additional' alternatives to banks and building societies *and* as 'substitutes' providing services for low-income people otherwise dependent on the whims of payday lenders and loan sharks.

In Hull, the evolving territorial politics of credit union development has worked at several levels. Initial attempts to promote a 'new' development model encouraged local credit union activists to discuss the potential for a more socially inclusive, city-wide common bond (Fuller 1998). However, for some activists this scalar shift was deeply problematic. There was a great reluctance to move away from the community development philosophy, contributing to divisions within the local credit union forum which was set up to assess the future development of the movement in Hull. There was a concern that smaller community credit unions would be absorbed into a larger, less personal, city-wide entity. Local people reliant on community credit unions for savings and loans would potentially be excluded from the new credit union model (Fuller 1998).

To some extent this scenario has been borne out with the merger and consolidation of community credit unions in the western half of the city into a larger city-wide financial institution, which in turn has expanded into rural areas outside the city boundaries. The Hull and East Yorkshire Credit Union (HEYCU) now serves a common bond area of 500,000 people and membership is based on work and residence. Around the time of its incorporation in 2002, HEYCU had 1,723 members and assets of £778,000. By 2010, HEYCU had grown to 7,251 members with savings of well over GBP £4 million (HEYCU 2010). It now offers a wide range of services including savings, loans (offered at 6.5% annual interest), income on savings interest, insurance, and child trust funds. Its common bond extends well beyond the Hull municipal boundaries to encompass a diverse rural and urban population. HEYCU has opened new branches in the surrounding rural towns of Driffield, Bridlington, Beverley and Goole. Perhaps more crucially, the Hull credit union now brands itself less as an institution of last resort serving only the financially excluded in the city but rather as very much part of the mainstream, offering a range of services that compete with local banks and building societies. In short, driven by national developments, the alternative nature of the credit union movement in Hull has been radically transformed along the lines of an alternative 'additional' enterprise.

REFLECTIONS AND CONCLUSIONS

In this chapter, I have argued that the re-positioning of British credit unions as alternative economic enterprises has been doubly determined by struggles within the movement for a wider presence in British society, and by the efforts of the UK state to ensure that credit unions can compete with mainstream financial institutions as well as with other less socially desirable 'alternatives'. There was never a moment when the alterity of credit unions was fixed in time and space; rather the nature of alterity has been negotiated and contested relationally over time at the national and local scales. This does not mean that we should not attempt to abstract from these dynamic processes and identify different conceptual categories to explain the alterity of alternative economic enterprises. Rather the challenge is to ensure that our concrete abstractions are always sensitive to territory and context.

Binary thinking about, for instance, the merits of two different credit union models should be rejected because it forecloses knowledge of alternative social structures which evolve relationally and territorially. Understanding how the alterity of economic enterprises evolves demands that we grapple with complex issues of territory, scale, the state, politics and regulation. The British credit union movement is a good example of this: the alternative nature of UK credit unions as social enterprises is intimately caught up in a strategic interplay between mainstream and oppositional forces working at the local, national and global scales. The purpose of this chapter has therefore been to develop new concrete abstractions around which knowledge of such alternatives can be further progressed.

Acknowledgements: Primitive versions of this chapter were presented at seminars held at the Katholische Universität Eichstätt-Ingolstadt, Germany, in January 2012 and at the Department of Geography, Kentucky University, USA, in April 2012. I am grateful to both institutions for inviting me and in particular to Hans-Martin Zademach, Sebastian Hillebrand, Andy Wood, Susan Roberts, Michael Samers and Amanda Fickey. Duncan Fuller was the inspiration for many of the ideas embodied in this chapter. The usual disclaimers apply.

The Alternative Economy at the Regional Scale? Lessons from the Chiemgau

Peter North and Katinka Weber

INTRODUCTION

Ever since Marx and Engels produced their famous critique of what they called 'utopian', as opposed to 'scientific' socialism, orthodox Marxist treatments of economic alterity have been concerned that such experiments are doomed to failure. For Marx and Engels, social change occurs not when some genius or other develops a perfect model for a future society, but through mass action when capitalism reaches the limits of its productivity. Further, ordinary people, Marx and Engels argued, do not have the resources to 'opt out' of capitalist economies for long periods, and if large numbers of people did attempt it, then the forces of the state would stop them (Engels 1892/1968). Economic alternatives are "interesting, but not compelling", and proponents of them are naïve, Pollyanna-ish romantics (Gibson-Graham 2002: 25). In short, experiments do little more than provide a brief glimpse of an alternative.

Marx and Engel's pessimistic conceptualisations notwithstanding, contemporary alternative currency networks have emerged in a number of localities over the past thirty years or so. While they vary from country to country, at their heart is a network, members of which exchange goods and services with a form of currency they issue and value locally. The currency might be like a banknote, a cheque, or just an entry on a computer. By 1999 there were 303 Local Exchange Trading Schemes (LETS) schemes in the UK (Williams et al. 2001), operating with mixed results (Aldridge and Patterson 2002). Here, LETS gave their currency a local name, like the Bobbin in Manchester, Tales in Canterbury, Favours in Bristol, Brights in Brighton. In Australia, Canada, and New Zealand the networks exchanged green dollars (North 2002). In France, local money schemes called local exchange systems (*Systeme de Exchange Local*, SEL – grains of salt) proliferated, in Hungary, Talente or *Kör* (circles) (North 2006b). In the United States time-based local currency in paper form re-emerged in towns like Great Barrington, Massachusetts, and Ithaca, New York (Maurer 2003).

Ithaca Hours inspired an Argentine NGO, the Programme for Local Self Sufficiency, to develop paper-based alternative currency networks that involved literally millions of users across Argentina during the first years of the 21st century (North 2007). The EF Schumacher Society's experiments in Great Barrington were presented to the emerging Transition Movement (Hopkins 2008), developing citizen based responses to concerns about peak oil, climate change and economic austerity as a tool for building what activists thought of as sustainable and resilient localised economies (North 2010b). Paper based local currencies were established in a number of transition towns. As economic crisis hits Greece and Spain, many are following the lead of Argentines in establishing barter clubs to meet basic needs in crisis situations (Donadio 2011; John 2012). And also in Germany several types of *Tauschringe* and more recently, *Regiogeld* (regional money) schemes are in operation (Schroeder 2006; Thiel 2011).

As alternative economic practices, subaltern currency networks now have some track record, yet experiences are mixed. There is evidence both for and against the core Marxist critique of utopian economic practices. They are more than 'dwarfish', but only in two places – Argentina at the turn of the 21st century, and currently in the German

Bundesland of Bavaria – have significant numbers of people been engaged in significant amounts of economic activity using alternative currencies. The extreme social and economic crisis that hit Argentina after December 2001 makes the networks there a special case, as arguably are the contemporary schemes in Greece and Spain. In this light, the success of the scheme in Bavaria deserves some special consideration in view of debates about 'capitalisms' as opposed to 'capital' (Peck and Theodore 2007). For instance, what is provoking debate in the UK as its economy struggles to come out of recession are questions around the usefulness of Rheinish capitalism such as that in Bavaria as an antidote to the pathologies of Anglo-Saxon neoliberal capitalism.

Can the UK learn from the region's specificities such as its inhabitant's strong regional identity, its local banks and its famous *Mittelstand* of family owned firms with longer investment time horizons and a stronger commitment to the health of the region (Studzinski 2013)? Having been united from a loose confederation of principalities and city states only in 1870, Germany also has a strong regional and local tradition that lasts to this day. Does German capitalism have something to say about conceptions of globalised capitalism and its power to reduce regional differences in economic forms (Gertler and Vinodrai 2005)? In particular, scholars look to the ways through which the *Mittelstand* is financed, especially by local and regional banks (Audretsch and Elston 1997). Can such alternative forms of financial institutions help to generate a vibrant community based sustainable economy? This chapter reports of findings from interviews with organisers and users of a regional currency in the Chiemgau region of South Bavaria.

THE EURO CRISIS AND REGIONAL CURRENCIES

The introduction of the Euro is a relatively new phenomenon, and given the crisis in the Eurozone there are concerns that a one-size-fits-all monetary policy set by the European Central Bank in Frankfurt cannot fit the diversity of local conditions from Latvia to Lisbon. In other words, the extent that the continent of Europe is what Mundell (1961) called an 'optimal currency area' where the benefits outweigh the costs is debatable. The argument for the Euro is that replacing national with a continent-wide currency would be more efficient by reducing transaction costs for trade across borders, leading to more trade and, it is claimed, greater welfare. It would be easier to compare prices across space, driving costs down, and less uncertainty about exchange rate fluctuation means that businesses can make long term plans. The result is less uncertainty about prices. Finally, opportunities for speculation on fluctuations between competing currencies will disappear, preventing otherwise functioning markets from being disrupted by herd behaviour. A bigger, more efficient market will encourage more trade, more inward investment, more efficient location decisions, thus more growth. All this results in improved human welfare (DeGrauwe 2000). National economic sovereignty, Eurozone enthusiasts argue, is a chimera in an age of globalisation where Europe must compete with the BRICs, and the benefits of integration outweigh any costs by far.

More radical left voices have seen the EU more as a vehicle for corporate neoliberal forms of globalisation than as a utopian internationalist project making war between European nations inconceivable (Baimbridge et al. 2006). Their concerns have focused on the single market as a tool for big business to reduce labour and environmental standards, on the growth and stability pact that accompanied the Euro as a tool for disciplining national economies that do not sign up to the Washington Consensus of balanced budgets and fiscal 'responsibility' and 'stability' above job creation and the protection of working people's living standards.

In another context, Dinerstein (2001), following Bonefeld and Holloway (1996), calls this the 'violence of stability'. Left critics argue that membership of the EU prescribes progressive nationalist projects like the UK Labour Left's Alternative Economic Strategy (Cripps et al. 1981) or 'Local Socialisms' of the 1980s (Boddy and Fudge 1984;

Mackintosh and Wainwright 1987), which looked to protect manufacturing industry from what we now know was the first wave of what Harvey (1992) called the 'spatial fix' of a crisis of capitalist productivity – the move of manufacturing to lower cost and lower regulated countries. The Cambridge economist Ha Joon Chang (2007) argues persuasively that weaker economies might want to protect and nurture their growing economic resources in much the same way as a family protects and nurtures its children: we expect them to pay their way at eighteen, but not at eight.

Greens share the left's charge that the EU is more of a vehicle for neoliberal forms of globalisation than for internationalism and solidarity, but their concerns focus more on the role of the single market in privileging big, global business over smaller local firms trading in local markets and thereby contributing to local distinctiveness (Scott Cato 2006). The concrete benefits to ordinary citizens – beyond more convenient ways to pay for European holidays – are less obvious. The single market, greens argue, leads to a bland, standardised 'clone town' economy (NEF 2010) dominated by global brands (Simms 2007). They also point to the absurdity of the carbon emissions and avoidable consumption of limited fuel resources associated with identical products produced in one country and transported to another to be sold: for example, Dutch butter sold in the UK and British butter sold in the Netherlands (Woodin and Lucas 2004). They argue for a greater commitment to local, more self-reliant economies over global trade (Douthwaite 1996; Shuman 2001; Cavanagh and Mander 2004). While attachment to the local should not be conflated with a commitment to autarky or to xenophobia, critics would argue that they underplay the benefits of international trade and communication associated with progressive conceptions of globalisation (North 2010a). This scepticism about European financial integration has led many greens who feel this way to promote local currencies as a methodology for strengthening local economies as an alternative to integration.

And it is in Bavaria that this alternative regional project has advanced the furthest.

GERMAN REGIONAL CURRENCIES

Building on the experiences and limitations of the German equivalent of LETS, the first German Regiogeld, the Roland in Bremen, was established in 2001, followed closely by the Chiemgauer in Bavaria. In 2008 there were 28 regional currencies across Germany. German Regiogeld is an attempt to build regional currencies that operate as a real alternative to the Euro, stimulating new regional production. They seek to maximise local purchasing power and to strengthen the local economy by binding money to the district or region, keeping it flowing within the community. Their general aim is to establish an atmosphere of cooperation, to facilitate sponsorship of local NGOs and community organisations, and to build an economy that includes less monetary speculation and, in order to reduce carbon emissions, entails less transport – especially of goods that can be produced anywhere as they do not depend upon specific local climatic conditions or resources.

There is a rich literature on German regional currencies not available in English. In what follows we draw on this literature to explore this regional dimension of experimentation with alternative currencies. Many authors discuss regional currencies in relation to an increasingly globally integrated economy and assess their possible contribution to fostering sustainable regional development (e.g. Bode 2004; 2005; Gelleri 2005; Herrmann 2005; 2006; Meßenzehl 2006; Paech 2008; Spehl 2008; Volkmann 2009).

Niko Paech (2008) is an advocate of regional currencies as ways to transition to a post-growth economy in order to avoid dangerous climate change. He argues that while critics generally acknowledge that complementary currencies do stimulate economic circulation within regions, in aggregate, he argues, they stifle growth, as businesses do not benefit from trading across regions; i.e. they do not benefit from economies of scale. In contrast with more conventional economic analyses, he regards this as a benefit, highlighting the ecological (constantly rising CO_2 emissions etc.) and human costs (e.g. consumerism, personal stress, unhappiness etc.) of a reliance on a growth economy and globalisation. Consequently, Paech sees regional currencies as a way to create socially inclusive, stable and ecologically more responsible economies, as "Regios [regional currencies] direct buying power from globalised markets to local economies, which strengthens the local demand for labour" (Paech 2008: 17).

Siglinde Bode (2004, 2005) considers the potential of regional currencies for the development of structurally weak regions within Europe, and in particular rural areas suffering from a lower density of inhabitants, few jobs for people with higher qualifications, high structural unemployment, and low income and capital among households. She argues that capital flows out of such regions as businesses settle in urban centres to take advantage of production facilities and infrastructure. Bode (2005: 5) argues that regional currencies may counteract such trends at least partly, by sparking off closed "regional economic circulation, to keep *Wertschöpfung* (added value) in the region". She contends that while it will hardly be possible or desirable to separate regional economies entirely from other markets and regions due to the existing high degree of economic integration, regional currencies provide a mechanism for regional actors through which they can manage, or direct their economic exchanges with centres in ways that suit them (2005: 8). Good, beneficial connections that strengthen and are welcomed by both parties can remain, while connections that funnel wealth from weaker to stronger regions can be managed, or even closed.

In a similar line of argument Herald Spehl (2008) highlights the potential import substitution effect of regional currency schemes, and linked to this, their potential to be part of an endogenous development strategy. As they lead consumers to buy more regional produce and the money is, in turn, spent with regional suppliers and service providers, there is a tendency to replace certain imports. The scope of this depends on the level of participation of local entrepreneurs and their ability to supply goods that previously had to be acquired outside the region (Spehl 2008: 22).

In turn, Eva-Maria Hubert (2007) focuses on regional currencies as a much neglected dimension of citizens' responses to problems within markets. Neoliberal analysts argue that there are limits to the effectiveness of state intervention, and advise a combination of deregulation and privatisation. In contrast, Hubert notes that in recent times citizen initiatives (including regional currency projects) have taken it upon themselves to deal with the problems of entrenched markets in the energy sector with practical, community-based entrepreneurial initiatives as alternatives to privatisation into the hands of the big energy companies (e.g. the community-based power station in Schönau or the energy cooperative in Delmenhorst). She argues that in a similar way, complementary currency schemes seek to "ensure regional economic circulation, promote the generation of added value in the region, strengthen small and medium-sized enterprises, and secure the basic supply [of goods and services] of the population in the region" (2007: 25). In addition, she argues that in this way civil society assists the state through corrective action to ensure a balance between the public and private sectors of the economy, in ways that strengthen communities rather than big business (2007: 27). This, she argues, secures a balanced economy for future generations.

Analysts of German regional currencies point to a set of economic advantages of such schemes. Firstly, they note that regional currency schemes encourage the formation and strengthening of networks between regional producers, suppliers, traders and consumers, as participants look for regional trading partners, perhaps replacing those futher away (Bode 2005: 7; Spehl 2008: 22). According to Bode (2005: 5, 7), this minimises capital flight as the surplus value generated through these chains stays within the region, allowing at least for a partial independence from the global economy.

Secondly, authors note that such schemes promote small and medium sized businesses, which already form the backbone of the regional economy (Bode 2005: 5). This, they argue, counteracts the entrenchment of regional markets, the merger of companies and formation of large business corporations. This is also beneficial as the latter are linked to a waste of resources and the reduction of local variety in businesses and goods (Hubert 2007: 25). The fact that businesses using regional currencies have access to a tool that enables them to withstand international competition, and are not under the same pressures to continually generate growth, means that relations between them, with their suppliers, and with their customers may be more 'cooperative' (Bode 2005: 8; Spehl 2008: 23), and competition may focus on ideas and innovations rather than on reducing costs, deregulation of labour or environmental standards, or increased levels of exploitation. In contrast, analysis argue that regional currencies may facilitate the creation of new lines of production (Bode 2005: 5, 7), including products and technologies suitable to smaller economic spheres (Herrmann 2006: 15). Moreover, they ensure variety, which is crucial to maintaining and increasing consumer sovereignty and freedom of choice. Hubert (2007) notes that while regional currencies disadvantage businesses which cannot for operational reasons participate in the initiative and may thus be suboptimal under the liberal free-market paradigm, their positive attributes outweigh this.

Thirdly, regional currency schemes may not only foster variety, but also resilience: they have the potential to secure the basic supply of goods and services to the population in the region, for instance, in case that transport networks are interrupted through disruptions in fuel supplies (Hubert 2007: 26). Spehl (2008: 23) highlights their potential in stimulating the decentralisation of energy supplies, which he sees as a necessary element of regional development in the light of rising energy costs, and adds that they may also decrease dependency on unsustainable fossil fuels and on nuclear energy which, post Chernobyl and Fukushima, raises obvious safety issues. Herrmann (2006: 15) provides some evidence for positive developments in this area, as well as for the thesis on the development of networks: stimulated by the Chiemgauer, the RegOel project in the Chiemgauer region supplies vegetable oil as fuel to farmers who are looking to find opportunities to spend their Chiemgauer. The initiative also managed to find a local company to convert tractors so that they could run on the oil.

Fourthly, authors argue that examples of regional currencies demonstrate their potential to raise levels of demand and supply in regional economies, which may also positively affect job opportunities and conversely lower unemployment. Hermann (2006: 15), for instance, notes that from April 2004, the year the *Sterntaler* (a regional currency in Berchtesgardener Land, a neighbouring region to Rosenheim and Traunstein) came into existence, until March 2005 the Sterntaler had created eleven jobs. Finally, some authors argue that they have the capacity to minimise the likelihood of economic crises in the future. This is as on the one hand because they are not subject to the speculative pressures that are integral to the globalised economy (Herrmann 2006: 15; also see Lietaer 2000: 111), and on the other, because economic processes are easier to grasp at a regional level, the outcomes of economic behaviour are visible much faster and risks can be dealt with more quickly (Herrmann 2006: 15). More-over, due to each participants' local knowledge and his/her personal sense of responsibility, there is a heightened social control and transparency of processes that generates added value (Hubert 2007: 25).

Beyond a consideration of the economic impacts of local currencies, authors also point to a set of positive social and environmental outcomes emerging from their use. A first issue they stress are the positive ecological effects given that regional, as opposed to globalised economic circulations entail shorter transport routes between production and market (Herrmann 2006: 15; Hubert 2007: 25; Spehl 2008: 22) relieving perhaps over congested transport networks. Here, regional circulations financially benefit the state, as road, train and shipping networks do not have to be expanded or strengthened (Hubert 2007: 26). Following on from this, authors highlight a second aspect, namely the potential educational aspect of the schemes, as participants come to support "the movement towards informed, environmentally friendly consumption" (Hubert 2007: 27). This contributes to personal development as participants are engaging with questions about "what money actually is, how one uses it, what type of consciousness relates to it" and "which types of development ... are linked to different types of money and their uses" (Spehl 2008: 23). The result is a more socially engaged citizenry, and markets that are socially inclusive as consumers respond adversely to pathological or antisocial behaviour on the part of the businesses they patronise.

A third set of positive social and environmental aspects of the schemes are their potential for "creating identities as well as the promotion of regional communities through the development of social networks" (Bode 2005: 9). In regional money schemes such as the *Chiemgauer* and the *Sterntaler,* users name a *Verein* (association) that will financially benefit from the use of the currency. Evidence from a study of these two schemes shows that currency users demonstrate an increased level of involvement in *Vereine,* and that through their engagement with the currency entrepreneurs knew more about *Verein* activities and those of other businesses involved (Herrmann 2006: 16). The opportunity to meet regularly further strengthens personal and business networks and their *Gemeinschaftsgefühl* (their feeling of community, or belonging together). Herrmann (2006: 16) notes that "you can also observe a heightened predisposition to cooperate between regional businesses and a strengthening of regional identity through RGIs [regional currency initiatives]. Therefore the regional currency has a strengthened information and communication function that the Euro does not exhibit". Consequently, these authors argue that these regional currencies strengthen local and regional social capital (Hubert 2007: 26; Spehl 2008: 23).

These accounts are extremely optimistic about the economic potential of regional currencies. Bode (2005: 9) argues that successful regional currencies could significantly "raise the attractiveness of regional living spaces", because of the variety of available "products and services, ecological qualities, diversified employment opportunities and the social and economic interrelations". Hubert (2007: 26) notes that in the light of a situation where market dynamics force individuals to be increasingly flexible and mobile, such schemes can "contribute to societal coherence and counteract the fragmentation of society", thus, he argues, addressing the existential loneliness which can make citizens susceptible to far right, populist and perhaps xenophobic political movements.

Despite these hopeful and positive evaluations, authors also point to obstacles to the realisation of the claimed potential of regional currencies. In an economic crisis, falling incomes may result in a lower aggregate regional buying power, especially in distressed regions. This may mean that economically constrained consumers are not prepared, perhaps not able, to pay a premium for potentially more expensive regionally-produced products. Moreover, it may be difficult to change existing patterns of consumption. The added value of regional currencies may need 'explanation', which involves a significant input of initiative and labour: "to gain a critical mass of transactions carried out in the regional currency, one has to have raised consciousness among a large mass of inhabitants" (Bode 2005: 8). And despite such efforts, competition between regions and with other global markets is likely to persist. This last point is partially supported by Muriel Herrmann's (2006: 15) findings in a study of the *Chiemgauer* and the *Sterntaler*. While entrepreneurs noted that as a result of their participation in the schemes, they spent more money in the region and felt that their participation had strengthened their comparative advantage against locally operating global businesses, she did not find evidence that a majority had switched to regional suppliers.

Many questions remain with regards to the scope and possibility of regional currencies. It remains to be seen, for instance, how far a region can realistically shed its dependency on globally produced products, what trading patterns emerge and how they affect the region, and how these may integrate the social and economic functioning of the economy (Bode 2005: 9). In particular, what is also not entirely clear is the extent that regional currencies can actually *build* regional networks, create consumer awareness, cooperation, solidarity and a *Gemeinschaftsgefühl*, and foster medium-sized businesses where they do not exist. How far is the pre-existence of (at least a minimum) of such elements in a region a pre-requisite for the success of a regional currency: is the existence of a strong regional currency a manifestation of, or a generator of, a strong regional economy composed of locally-owned banks, businesses, food and power production? A crucial factor is also the consideration of what geographical area must constitute a 'region' in order for schemes to operate successfully. All this must also be considered in relation to the economic rules and regulations behind regional currency schemes. We can discuss these issues with a consideration of the actually existing experience of Germany's most successful regional currency in the Chiemgau, Bavaria.

CHIEMGAUER

It is in the Chiemgau that we see the potential benefits of regional currencies discussed above realized to their greatest potential to date. Chiemgauer regional money circulates in an area of 100 kilometres around the lake Chiemsee in the south east of Bavaria. The aim is for Chiemgauer to circulate in an area small enough to have some coherence, regional identity and to be considered 'local', but big enough to include a wide enough variety of businesses that enough people use it for day-to-day purchases such that it makes a difference to the health of the local economy, and makes it possible to reduce emissions associated with transporting goods needlessly from place to place. This is achieved by working at a geographical scale large enough to facilitate enough business circulation that, the hope is, the average user of the currency can buy 50% of his or her requirements with it.

Secondly, Chiemgauer aims to circulate at a greater velocity than the Euro. Chiemgauer builds on a long history of monetary reforms based on the ideas of Austrian Rudolf Steiner and the Argentine-German money reformer Silvio Gesell (1958), who developed arguments in favour of the abolition of interest and for 'free money'. Gesell identified interest as the prime pathology of the capitalist system, and advocated interest-free banking. His ideas inspired the so-called *Frei-wirtschaft* (free economy) movement in post-World War One Germany, which established the *Wära-Tauschgesellschaft* (Wära Exchange

Association; the expression Wära comes from the German words for currency, *Währung*, and goods, *Ware*). The movement issued its own currency notes, interest free as a response to Germany's financial collapse and subsequent experiences of hyperinflation after the punitive post war Versailles settlement (Fisher 1933).

With the arrival of the depression in 1929 the owner of a coal mine in Schwanenkirchen, Bavaria used Wära notes to reopen his mine, with the Wära passed on to local merchants, then to the wholesalers, then on to the manufacturers who returned to the coal mine for coal. Gesell-inspired scrip notes issued by local authorities or business associations spread to other towns in Germany, Austria and Switzerland. In 1932, the town of Wörgl, Austria, used them to fund public works for unemployed people who spent the notes with local merchants. In turn, these merchants returned the notes back to the local authority as payment for local taxes, before being passed on again by the municipality to unemployed people (Dauncey 1988: 282n). Local state employees were paid 50% of their salary in scrip, inscribed with the words "They alleviate want, give work and bread". The notes could be exchanged for cash, but a service charge was levied that was greater than the costs of passing the note on.

Stamp scrip took on Gesell's ideas for *demurrage:* scrip could be banked or spent locally like ordinary cash, but it had to be 'validated' with a stamp purchased each week. After 52 weeks the note could be exchanged for cash by the local authority, using the receipts of the weekly stamps. If the note was not passed on, the holder of the note would still have to purchase the weekly stamps or the note would be worthless, so it was obviously in his or her interest to purchase something with it rather than hold on to it. Demurrage was intended to increase the velocity of circulation, as 'slow money', horded rather than spent, was regarded as the cause of the depression. The politics of the Wörgl notes are clear from the inscription on the back of the scrip:

"To all. Slowly circulating money has thrown the world into an unheard of crisis, and millions of working people are in a terrible need. From the economic viewpoint, the decline of the world has begun with horrible consequences for all. Only a clear recognition of these facts, and decisive action can stop the breakdown of the economic machine, and save mankind from another war, confusion and dissolution ... Men live from the exchange of what they can do. Through slow money circulation this exchange has been crippled to a large extent, and thus millions of men (sic) who are willing to work have lost their right to live in our economic system. The exchange of what we can do must, therefore, be again improved and the right to live regained for all of those who have been cast out." (Fisher 1933: 25)

The free economy movement then was centred on the area where south Germany, Austria and Switzerland meet – the Chiemgau. Drawing on Gesell's inspiration and the legacy of local currency experimentation in these three German speaking lands, the Chiemgauer adopted demurrage. It 'ages' or 'rusts' 2% per quarter of a year; 8% per year. Every quarter, those holding the notes must buy a sticker to be attached to each note, costing two cents per Chiemgauer. As no one wants to have to pay the cost of the sticker themselves, the incentive is to spend it before the due date. Local activists argue that as a consequence the local currency circulates three times faster than the Euro.

Clearly reflecting Steiner's influence, the Chiemgauer was developed as a Steiner school project through which the school hoped to strengthen connections with and boost sponsorship from local businesses. Believing that the conventional money system does not work well for small businesses, the school students worked with local companies to develop the project over three years, until it became an independent project in 2005 and the organiser Gelleri left the school to work full time on the Chiemgauer currency. Christian Gelleri's role and trusted status within the community was important. As a shopkeeper who was an active user of Chiemgauer put it:

"It works relatively well here because there is somebody behind it, Mr. Gelleri ... He does the publicity for the Chiemgauer, he supports it, he organises information events. He tries to recruit companies that participate, so there is very aggressive advertising behind it, too. That is why it works so well here."

Gelleri has been proactive in making sure that business users of the currency have been supported. He visits businesses regularly to troubleshoot and explain the Chiemgauer and its workings in a way that as another regular user put it "one really understands it, so that one ends up having a really good feeling doing it". Gelleri was described as having the empathy to be able to explain the concept to potential businesspeople, and this was an important aspect in the decision to use it.

As the project developed, five district offices were set up, through which Chiemgauer could be issued and redeemed. By 2013 there were 66 issuing points, including a number of voluntary and community associations. The currency is linked at parity to the Euro, meaning that the complications associated with linking the currency to time are avoided. It is issued in notes denominated 1, 2, 5, 10, 20 and 50 Chiemgauer, printed on special banknote paper and with 14 security features. Local images are printed on the notes, nodding to local pride. Users of the Chiemgauer buy them from an issuing office or non-profit-making agency, spending them with the more than 600 participating businesses. Voluntary and community associations that act as issuing agents can buy 100 Chiemgauer for 97 Euro, keeping the balance when they issue them to others. Businesses themselves can spend them with other businesses or non-profit-makers, or redeem them for Euros at one of the district offices. If they do the latter, they get 95 Euro for every 100 Chiemgauer. 2% of the deduction is used to fund the programme, while 3% goes to fund and support local *Vereine*. This support – currently, 260 Vereine are involved in the programme – is a major attraction. A chemist who accepted Chiemgauer put it thus:

"It is fun because you have an association that you support, a Verein, so you have this feeling of reward when you do your purchase. You have a more positive experience. So you have your club, in my case it is a rowing club which is just being established in Rosenheim, and I support it with the percentages. And I find that positive; it gives you a good feeling."

A debit card has been introduced with the result that an average of 35% of Chiemgauer transactions are electronic, with some popular businesses processing 80% of their Chiemgauer transactions in electronic form. The move from paper to card reader was funded with a regional development grant, and managed in cooperation with cooperative and state banks. The involvement of the local banks makes day to day use of the local currency easier. One respondent said:

"We have a cafe opposite us and I can buy my coffee and cake there with my Chiemgauer, if I want to; I can spend it in the organic market, in the shop; but because we get a lot of Chiemgauer we take most of them to the bank. The Sparkasse, the largest bank in Rosenheim also cooperates in with the Chiemgauer and offers Chiemgauer customers a bank account for free. So you can take the money there and then swap it back into Euros. I can't spend thousands of Chiemgauer in other shops each month ... In the past this was much more complicated. You had to swap the Chiemgauer in small bookshops, in small shops. In the past it was much more exotic. But now, the manager of the Chiemgauer organisation has taken a very good step by taking on the Sparkasse and they cooperate with him. The Sparkasse Rosenheim is a very large institution, not in terms of their financial turnover, but in the sense that they have a very large customer base. You can now get Chiemgauer there and swap them back ... This is a very good and easy solution, good service ... If I have a thousand Euros in my till, I can also take along the Chiemgauer, there really is no difference, really great ... You go to the same [bank] counter and then it's done."

This is evidence for the thesis that Germany's local banks support the generation of regional economic activity: but it is not to say that they necessarily supported radical innovations like Chiemgauer. Gelleri responds that at first they were resistant, and he had to work with an ethical, not a local bank. Only in time did the *Sparkasse* become involved, once demonstrable successes had been achieved.

The Chiemgauer local currency scheme is notable for its rigorous collection of data on how the currency circulates, and the way this data is made public. In December 2009, around 2,500 consumers a month changed 100,000 Euro a month into Chiemgauer, which produced 3,000 Chiemgauer for non-profit-makers. Some 98,000 Chiemgauer a month are eventually returned to the issuing offices, but only after they have circulated around the community. 70% of Chiemgauer are spent again, not redeemed. In 2009, 314,516 Chiemgauer were in circulation, having risen to 675.799 in 2013. Based on a sample of participating businesses, the project claims that since its inception Chiemgauer has turned over the equivalent of 8.6 million Euro, of which 3.9 million was in 2008, up to 5 million in 2010 and 6 million in 2011.

STRENGTHENING REGIONAL PRODUCTION

Gelleri argues that one third of the trades facilitated by Chiemgauer, worth the equivalent of some 600,000 Euro, is trade that would not otherwise have happened, and which strengthens the local economy. For example, food shops prefer local apples as they can pay for them with Chiemgauer, which has stimulated local apple production. Apple juice is no longer imported from North Germany. Money stays local, and is used to facilitate more production. A circle with a radius of 70 to 100km seems to combine 'local' with enough of a range of production to make enough goods and services purchasable with the currency. This conception of the 'local' is conceptualised in bioregional, not human administrative terms. It is also a pragmatic decision. Production should be as local as possible, with regards to consumer choice. Asked when a given product stops being 'local', we got the following response from the manager of a small organic supermarket that accepted Chiemgauer:

"We do try to stay within Germany with the products, where it works. So we would never import milk from England or buy butter from Poland, we would never buy eggs from Russia. What is produced in Germany, we buy in Germany, what is produced in the region, we buy in the region; everything else that you cannot get, we have to buy in ... Austria belongs to the region. ... We have our headquarters in Trostberg, we took a compass [and] we said 100km surrounding Trostberg is the region and Austria is [therefore] part of it."

Given that an active user of Chiemgauer currencies can meet most of his or her needs, this seems to be an acceptable bargain between conceptions of the local, and economic efficiency. Thoughtful businesses understand that the more people who accept the Chiemgauer, the greater will be the possibility that they can spend all the currency they earn, it stays local, and the business will attract repeat business. They put it thus:

"We hope that the customers [who use the Chiemgauer] buy more, or actually come here more often. That they think, 'I like it there' and that they come back. Maybe they would not come at all, if we did not accept the Chiemgauer."

As already indicated, the Chiemgauer can be changed back to Euros with a discount of 5%. This amount seems to be high enough to encourage businesses to try to spend the currency, but low enough that the business feels comfortable that it will not lose too much if it has to reconvert stocks of unspendable regional currency back into Euros. One respondent, the manager of an organic supermarket, explained how this works:

"We specialise in engaging small (local) suppliers because we are a regional bio (ecological/organic) retailer. We try to get as many products as possible from within the region ... Our company was founded in line with [the idea] of commercialisation of regional products and everything that's associated with this. So we search for producers that produce good quality products and we try to convince them to change their production to bio (ecological) products. So we have somebody who was a bio (ecological) inspector, and we go around and say 'listen, you have a great product, change to ecological production for us'; this also means that we buy his products, we naturally then also try to get him to use the Chiemgauer, so everything that has to do with regional commercialisation, including the Chiemgauer, we are trying to let this grow within the region ... We have to be pro-active and say 'we look for it, and this is how we want it'. We have 25 to 30 small suppliers and five wholesalers that supply us with the standard range and the rest we do ourselves."

This active user of Cheimgauer recognised the added value of the local.

"We are trying to market the products from the region, they are qualitatively better, cost more, the customers know that, we explain to the customers why this is. We say that the man behind [this product] is a one-man business. ... It is all produced through artisan techniques. The customers appreciate this, because they know who is behind the product."

STRONG SOCIAL CAPITAL AND 'EMBEDDEDNESS'

Does the currency work so well because the environment within which it circulates is conducive to it? Chiemgau is a very wealthy part of Bavaria, a part with a strong regional identity. Respondents said:

"It is a region of strong growth. Take the house prices for example here in Upper Bavaria: in Bavaria, there is a distinct north-south divide; if you look at Franken, from the northern part of Bavaria, towards south, the further south you get into the Alpine region there is a big population pressure ... In addition, we have very low unemployment figures."

Respondents also pointed to the high quality of life in the region: "It's the leisure value, it's the mountains, the lakes, the proximity to Munich, to Italy, to Salzburg."

In addition, they pointed to a strong tradition of mutual aid:

"They say that the farmer here builds his house with friends. But really, I have a helped a friend of mine who is farmer to put the roof on ... Ten of us helped him to put the tiles on the roof. That is really very rural and I think that you have to experience it from that kind of angle."

The Chiemgauer's success builds on and now strengthens a strong tradition of regional sourcing and regional cooperation of businesses, which is typical for most of southern Germany. Rural Bavaria has successfully resisted the destruction of small businesses by 'big box' and chain stores. Chiemgauer users feel that the local character matters:

"Well, this certainly plays a role. I am from Baden-Württemberg. I was very surprised when I moved to Bavaria four years ago, how it really works here with all the social networks. Baden-Württemberg is not really known for that; I don't really think that it [a regional currency] would work there ... Many people that live here simply support their region, thus they support the regional currency."

Perhaps what the Chiemgauer does best is to manifest this type of social capital to outsiders. This respondent went on to talk about regional currencies in other parts of Germany, for example in the Black Forest. He noted that they have some trouble establishing themselves, arguing: "the people there are different; they did not really have the enthusiasm".

An obvious barrier to the attractiveness of a new form of currency linked to the Euro is that potential users need first to decide that they want to use a new form of currency, and then make the decision to proactively to go to one of the issuing stations to change Euros into Chiemgauer, which might not be convenient. Further, prospective users are asked to change Euros, universal money that can be spent every-where, into Chiemgauer, which cannot. What is the incentive? There is no clear benefit apart from an altruistic or political commitment to your community and region and the chance to endow your favourite volun-tary organisation. So in all likelihood, it is the pre-existence of strong local Bavarian culture means that it is more likely that people will be well disposed to something that strengthens that culture. Consequently, even in this region the attraction is not universal: it is only to those who value such aspects who participate in the scheme. One informant, running a business that had five Chiemgauer customers a day out of an overall customer base of up to 500 a day argued:

"It is a very specific group of customers; we will not make this system fit for the masses, for that there are too few conscientious consumers. I do believe that very specific people support this scheme ... It is not necessarily something for the masses, because the people are far too comfortable to have two types of cur-rency in their wallet; to have another bank account for the Chiemgauer. The so-cial commitment of the people is unfortunately not big enough to do that ... I think that we have to free ourselves from the idea that it leads to a large turno-ver, but the interesting thing is the structure of the customer base."

'RUSTING' – PROBLEMS AND OPPORTUNITIES

From a conventional economic perspective written for the German Bundesbank, economist Gerhard Rösl (e.g. 2005; 2006a; 2006b) has argued that the danger that follows is Gresham's law: 'bad money forces out good'. If customers decide to spend ('inferior', local) Re-giogeld and keep ('superior', universal) Euros in the bank they are effectively moving Euros out of circulation, and if this was taken too far it might lead to a drought of Euros and an 'inferior' supply of money.

In this situation, a business might end up in a position whereby it has to accept a currency that is not accepted everywhere and which the business cannot itself re-circulate, instead of the universal currency it would otherwise have accepted and can spend. If this is the case and if these businesses are already operating with tight margins, then this can be hurting the very people you want to help – a perverse effect of a local currency scheme. The solution would be the business limiting the amount of Regiogeld it accepts to a manageable amount, perhaps seeing it as a discount promotion bringing in some new customers. But this would rather miss the wider point. This exchange, in an organic supermarket that carried out some 10% of its turnover, illustrates the debate. This business spent large amounts of Chiemgauer, and did not lose 5% through demurrage or changing back:

"We have to use it within a year. So, either I leave it in my bank account where it remains for a year and then I lose 5%, or I spend it within the year (and) I do not lose anything. Because we take the Chiemgauer in the shop as payment we can also pay our regional suppliers with Chiemgauer, so it remains in circulation ... We say: 'Well, we buy that much from you, let's say for two-thirds Euros, one-third Chiemgauer', so that we can also get rid of ours; so that we can get the circulation going ... We ask our wholesalers 'Can we pay in Chiemgauer? Do you have suppliers that you can pay with Chiemgauer?' ... We also have small bakers that produce bread for us who say 'Well, two-thirds Euro, one-third Chiemgauer', so that the circulation can be sustained ... There are many shops here that accept the Chiemgauer, that's to say, our suppliers can get rid of their money. Only if it builds up, if a single person gets a huge amount of Chiemgauer this can be a problem."

Q: And in time, what if your suppliers said: more Euros, less Chiemgauer?

"Yes, that can happen, if it gets too much then they say that ... The last one who has no one which would accept the Chiemgauer, that's the one who loses. [But] for example, if we take apple juice, the person who produces the apple juice might spend a bit in the cafe, might bring it back here to buy goods from you, so it goes round again, or buys some shoes ... It's not that you end up the last in the chain."

Of course, many business owners and customers never see the value of a local currency. Comments from non-users included:

"I take all the credit cards, why do more? ... Not many people use them."
"People don't want it, why compete further?"
"Customers demanded credit cards so I got them, they aren't demanding Chiemgauer. If they did I'd do it. But there is no demand, so why do it?"

An interesting perspective comes from a 200 year old shoe shop that sells locally-made shoes, the sort of business Chiemgauer users might be attracted to, and one that might share the Chiemgauer ethos of strengthening local production. The owner was articulate in his opposition; to the question whether he used Chiemgauer was a loud "No!". He explained that his business is founded on local trade anyway, he did not want to grow it further, and he did not want to be 'coerced' into accepting Chiemgauer. He argued "I have enough on my plate keeping a business going without dealing with that. It's a hassle: why do it? I buy from local businesses anyway." Similarly, other businesses could feel:

"Some customers very much support the currency and think it is a good thing, while others perceive it as a hassle, because of the way the money has to be handled; i.e. that you have to buy a certain amount, that you have to keep topping up its value, and that you lose 5% when you swap it back into Euros. Many customers find this too complicated."

Even future supporters argued: "I was skeptical because I was thinking about the administrative efforts, the additional work; you have to count them along with your cash. You have your cash and then you have something else; you have to document it in your books and count it. That means that there is automatically more work. So I was skeptical at first." It took the persistence of Christian Gelleri to overcome this reticence.

CONCLUSIONS

We know that regional currencies in Germany circulate at the regional scale, which seems to be a large enough scale to enable businesses to spend the Regiogeld they take in, and customers to meet 50% of their needs using alternative currency schemes. Chiemgauer circulate in a wealthy part of Germany with a strong regional identity, a tradition of "doing things differently", and strong social capital. So, is the success of regional currencies dependent on a pre-existing network of locally-owned, independently-minded businesspeople and local banks? Or, can a local currency help *build* such a local infrastructure where it doesn't currently exist?

While we cannot yet provide a definite answer to the question, our findings indicate that the pre-existence of these factors is important to the scheme's success. Moreover, the involvement of local banks seems to have had an important legitimising effect, and made transactions smoother, so we do see fairly large scale usage of an alternative economic project. As has been noted, crucial is also the role of Gelleri himself, a locally well-known, well-connected and charismatic character who is prepared to put labour into the scheme and drives the education aspect. His efforts to convince citizens and business owners of the scheme's viability are evidently important.

Critical perspectives on regional currencies from an orthodox perspective assume that 'universal' currency is superior and a local currency is inferior just because you cannot spend it everywhere. It is a perspective wedded to globalisation, ignoring the fuel burnt and carbon emitted in the process. The arguments for transitioning towards a more localised low carbon economy are not on the radar. Chiemgauer seems to have broken out of this trap by circulating at a scale that means enough businesses accept it to enable them to spend on their Regiogeld with their suppliers. Gelleri indicated that a next step is to deepen this process by boosting the amount of local production, through Chiemgauer loans. This would foster new businesses to carry out import substitution. The process should be followed closely and the scheme deserves further scholarly attention to see whether local resilience is genuinely strengthened through regional currencies.

The Possibilities of Economic Difference? Social Relations of Value, Space and Economic Geographies

Roger Lee

INTRODUCTION

"Craft Fair[s] ... are all over the place ... this year. Every school and church hall is hosting one, for which – geographically and horologically bounded as I am ... – I am very grateful.

A craft fair feels like the optimal level for capitalism. I'm happy that we've moved away from barter – because ... I have very short arms and there's a very definite number of piglets I could carry to market ... – but ... anything bigger than a market stall is too much concentration of capital ... how much better we'd all be (literally and metaphorically) if money still came in gold coins and got stored in boxes and leather bags until it was time to spend it again ...

Think how much happier we'd all be if business was conducted face to face." (Lucy Mangan 2011: 10)

In this passage, from an article in the weekend magazine section of a UK national newspaper, the journalist Lucy Mangan writes an economic geography of difference: different spaces, different times, different money. Idealistic but also unrealistic, it captures many of the contradictions of localized and apparently utopian economies. The advantages of accessibility and face-to-face transactions in localized economies are clear but questions of production do not figure and of finance only by ignoring the advantages and convenience (geographical and horological) of an effective financial, to say nothing of a credit-system. Above all – and as with so many popular and business-press accounts of capitalism – it treats capitalism as an unproblematic, even natural, given or, at least, as a given with only surficial contradictions.

In this it is not unusual. Idealism tends to trump realism in discussions of economic difference. So a first step in developing a hopefully more convincing account of the possibilities for economic change is to recognize some of the realities of all economies and the particularities of capitalist economies. This paper considers the nature of, and the possibilities for, alternative forms of economic geographies. It does so by pursuing a number of arguments concerning the simultaneous sociality and materiality of economic geographies and the inescapable significance of both in any consideration of economy/economic geography, the political significance of the mutual formation of territorial and relational space and the notion that economic change is necessarily profound and becomes possible, perhaps, only through crisis.

The permanence of economic geographies (however dynamic that permanence/those economic geographies may be) is difficult to transform beyond materially, socially and spatially narrow limits. This is due not least to the material infrastructure and relations necessary to enable economic activity and, even more significantly, to the entrenched power relations which shape both the nature of economic geographies and the material landscapes through which they take place. And the inescapable significance of these material and social relations raises, in turn, questions of the extent to which economic geographic difference is sustainable and generalisable across space and through time. One such question provides the primary focus of what follows: Is it possible to avoid parochialist economies and politics in the construction of economic alternatives?

However, the chapter offers very few answers to this question and is restricted merely to one possible frame through which some answers may become possible. Central to the argument in what follows is the notion of what I like to call 'the ordinary economy' (Lee 2006, 2010a). And it is the ideas which shape my understanding of the ordinary economy that inform much of what follows here. But before considering these arguments and their consequences, a more immediate question concerns the question of diversity, alternatives and otherness in economic activity.

DIVERSITY, ALTERNATIVES AND OTHERNESS IN ECONOMIC ACTIVITY

These three words are often used interchangeably in discussions of what J.K. Gibson-Graham (1996 2006) refers to as thinking the economy otherwise. However they have distinct if overlapping meanings and the order in which they are listed here indicates an ascending degree of difference. Diversity implies the co-presence of various strands of difference. The notion of variegated capitalism has been explored by Peck and Theodore (2007) and they point up a long history of, for example, the recognition of diverse forms of capitalism and of arguments around the superiority of one or the other. These debates illustrate very effectively the issue of the permanence and the limited possibilities for change in economic relations alluded to in the introduction to this paper. Clearly, the alternatives identified in such debates are real and they produce real economic difference but they are all variations on a theme (of capitalism) and so indicate limited difference.

At least three meanings of 'alternatives' overlap in economic discourse. The first suggests the possibility and/or the presentation of choice of economy/economic geography. This is, as just suggested, not a notion that the permanence of economies can embrace very easily – except, perhaps, over the long term. A good example would be the constraints on the implementation of even self-serving environmental modifications to economic behaviour. More conventionally – and, for some (e.g. Harvey 2000), more realistically – the idea of 'alternative' refers to a mutual exclusivity. This is a form of critique which J.K. Gibson-Graham (1996; 2006) rightly rails against in her ever more profound exposure of the simplistic and unquestioning acceptance of the defining norms of capitalism which, once accepted, then shape all ensuing argument. A third notion of alternative – one which, arguably, informs much of the work in this field (see, for example, Fuller et al 2010b) – concerns the formulation of lifestyles, culture, art forms ... considered as preferable to those of contemporary mainstream society. These alternatives often involve less conventional, less materialistic and less institutionalised economies more in harmony with nature. And they are often localised in scale.

The question of economic otherness raises the possibility of the most profound critique of mainstream accounts and practices of economy. At its weakest, however, otherness may refer simply to a remainder, what is left over – those features of economy hardly considered fundamental to its ongoing dynamic and so open to experimentation without any great threat to mainstream ideas. It may also refer to additional/further possibilities arising from existing arrangements. Such might include, for example, extensions or minor modifications like notions of regulation or the insertion of democratic possibilities into economic behaviour. Much conventional economic debate revolves around this notion of other including, for example, arguments for the greater/lesser involvement of the state in shaping economic activity. However, both these aspects of other are necessarily defined by what is not other. That is to say, they usually refer to a benchmark given by mainstream economic relations and so fall foul of the Gibson-Graham critique in failing to get beyond existing relations and concepts. But otherness can also refer to much more powerful notions of the delimitation or constitution of a superior self as distinct from an inferior other. An example of such might be an economy defined and practised with people as its subjects rather than its objects.

However, leading on from this idea of a self defined by an other, otherness may refer to a definition of difference and to the social construction of boundaries of social inclusion and exclusion rigorously policed in both ideological and material terms. Despite the apparent power of economic 'globalisation', geo-political examples of such distinctions abound in the contemporary world. A particularly pernicious example of the contemporary neo-liberal geographical imagination is the increasingly oppressive terms of contemporary norms and policies around immigration balancing neuroses associated with fears of the other with the practical benefits for capital of cheap labour. And within the neo-liberal state, the ideology which constructs poverty as fault and blame allows the demonisation of the poor and supports their exclusion from the welfare norms of a civilized society.

It also leads to nonsensical (not to say immoral) economic policies. If growth is considered a worthwhile objective, capital must be subsidized – via tax breaks and avoidance, for example – in order to offset the lack of demand emanating from the failure to pay at least a living wage to large swathes of the working population. But, of course, provided that the marginalisation and increased vulnerability of the poor is considered to be an adequate means of social discipline and control, this is an excellent policy for the further enhancement of the economically powerful – both a tiny minority of well-paid workers and, more especially, certain forms of capital (which, given the nature of such policies, would exclude retail capital and large portions of production capital).

STRATEGIC ESSENTIALISM AND THE CELEBRATION OF DIFFERENCE

Clearly, notions of economic diversity, alternatives and otherness cut both ways. They do not necessarily lead in progressive directions. And, insofar as they do, they are frequently constrained in size and geographical and temporal reach. As indicated above, one objective of this paper is to query this apparent stalemate and to ask whether there are ways of (re)thinking economy which might have greater purchase in extending and sustaining progressive difference. One way into this may be via notions of strategic essentialism and their problematic relations with the celebration of difference – as advocated by, for example, Iris Marion Young (1990).

Of course, an immediate problem here is that pernicious notions of otherness are encouraged by a political economy designed to increase inequality not only further to benefit the self of capital and privilege but to marginalise the other of low paid and under-valued engagement in economic activity or of no engagement at all. Gender, race, religion, the immigrant other etc. are used not only to divert attention from the social relations of capitalism as the crucial drivers of poverty, inequality and power(lessness) but to prevent or obstruct the possibilities of the practices of strategic essentialism in exploiting what is common to all the oppressed in opposing the systematic processes of uneven development which generates their oppression in the sustenance of capitalism.

In such a context, the question which lies at the heart of what follows is simply 'can the ordinary economy act, somehow as a (partial) resolution of this contradiction?' This paper does not pretend to offer an answer to this question but considers (at least some of) the circumstances in which an answer may be sought. A first step is to acknowledge the non-reducible material features of economic geographies whilst at the same time recognizing the inseparability of their material and social relations and the decisive role of the latter in the practice of economic activity.

SPATIALITIES OF CIRCUITS OF VALUE

There is something irreducibly material, irreducibly social and irreducibly geographical about economies/economic geographies (Lee 2006, 2011). And these three features are closely linked. Economic geographies are the geographies constructed by people in their struggle to make a living. They are the essential and inescapable geographies through which economies take place. Constituted of circuits of value –

which necessarily involve the incessant movement and transformation of value from consumption via exchange to production and then via exchange to consumption – economies/economic geographies are simultaneously territorial and relational. Not only do they all exist within particular territorial geographical settings but they create relational geographies in order to exist. Such relational geographies both shape and are shaped by territorial geographies of place.

Thus these geographies – places and spaces – are not only the essential conditions of existence of economies but also the objectives (the expansion, extraction and recirculation of value) of the movement and transformation involved in circuits of capital (hence my insistence on the term 'economic geographies' rather than mere 'economies' which cannot exist (see Lee 2002). Upon the possibilities of such spatial and temporal repetition is all social life materially predicated. And the material coherence and effectiveness – autonomy – of economies/ economic geographies is inescapable if social life is to be sustained. All genuinely autonomous (that is to say self-maintained) economic geographies must at minimum maintain such material sustenance. This involves the repeated production, circulation and consumption of adequate quantities and qualities of value to sustain human being across space and through time. Indeed, it is this requirement of material sustenance across space and time which offers the most significant criterion for defining what economic geographies might be. This is what, following Stuart Hall (1998) and Dave Featherstone (1998), I call "determination in the first instance by the economic". It is de-termination in the first instance because it is inescapable. But – and this is crucial socially and hence politically – it is not the last word.

Circuits of value cannot be understood in merely material terms. They are simultaneously both social and material. Whilst they may take on the appearance of material flows of value through consumption, exchange and production, the nature, trajectory and purpose of these flows are shaped – and their sustainability defined as much by social relations of value (compare Figures 1 and 2) as by their material coherence and logistics. Social relations of value are the shared, con-

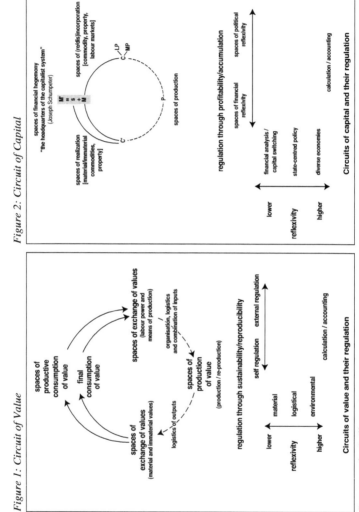

Figure 2: Circuit of Capital

Figure 1: Circuit of Value

Source: author's illustrations

tested, or imposed understandings about the nature, norms and purposes of circuits of value. They make sense of, give direction to and, above all, define the parameters and the criteria of evaluation of circuits of value. Figure 1 is therefore a practical impossibility as it abstracts from the social relations which drive such circuits. Figure 2 represents a capitalist circuit of value in which the social relations of capital (labour-capital relations) and the evaluative capitalist imperative of the production of surplus value and its accumulation shape its trajectory.

Circuits of capital (circuits of value shaped and driven by capitalist social relations of value) are focused on accumulation and profitability measured relentlessly and dispassionately by what Schumpeter calls 'the headquarters of the capitalist system'. Despite the profound financial crisis which began in 2007, these headquarters are concentrated ever more influentially within the financial system and its loci within the major financial centres of the global economic geography. The concentrated and intensively developed financial division of labour enabled in these centres exerts the dominant and decisive influence on the trajectory of capitalist circuits of value. What matters is what is deemed necessary to maximize surplus value. This objective is imposed by the ability of financial centres to switch capital from one place to another, one time to another and one activity to another, often in the twinkling of an eye.[1]

Figures 1 and 2 emphasise the movement and transformation of value across space and through time inherent to circuits of value and their economic geographies. But circuits also require at least temporary spatial fixity – at least of the movements involved – to enable the consumption, exchange and production of value to take place. It is this

---

1   Of course, I recognize that the financial crisis has exposed not only such power relations but also the ability to manipulate them to gain massive quantities of economic rent (often in a corrupt and certainly crazily risky fashion) on the part of the agents involved in the financial system.

complex of relationships between movement / relationality, fixity / territoriality, materiality / sociality and pitiless financial evaluation, along with the logistics of the material manifestations of economic geographies which lie at the problematic heart of the establishment of 'diverse', 'alternative' or 'other' forms of economic geography.

ECONOMIC GEOGRAPHIES OF ECONOMIC DIFFERENCE

Just as it is possible to discern various notions of difference, so too is it possible to distinguish between varying forms of difference in economic geographies. All circuits of capital, even the most apparently globalised (Dicken 2011) and virtual are founded in and through places and the territorial and relational geographies which constitute them. In this sense, then, all economic geographies (however defined and delimited) are different. And, as Peck and Theodore (2007) have shown, capitalist economic geographies are highly differentiated not least around the axes of regulation. More rare, at least in terms of spatial and temporal extent are genuinely democratised economic geographies – and this rarity illustrates the point stressed above that whilst it is possible to describe and think of economic geographies of difference, such as those postulated by Lucy Mangan, for example, it becomes extremely difficult to identify spatially and temporally large-scale instances of such economies.

Rather, economic difference tends to be associated with the local. Examples here might include what Raymond Williams (1989) refers to as militant particularism which, however militant they may be, frequently remain locked into capitalist circuits (e.g. Harvey and Hayter 1993) and rarely become autonomous economic geographies – at least in the terms in which such economic geographies are defined above. Whilst the militancy and the sheer uncomfortable, difficult and frequently reviled work involved in the construction of such geographies is aimed at the transformation of economic geographies into practices for people rather than merely by people, the question which is frequently begged becomes whether it is possible to go beyond militant particularism to achieve genuine and genuinely autonomous economic difference. This paper concludes by exploring the possibilities presented by the 'ordinary economy' in contributing to and extending militant particularism.

THE ORDINARY ECONOMY AND THE RESOLUTION OF PAROCHIALISM?

Much of the work of David Harvey over the years has been directed at inserting geography into historical materialism, historical-geographical materialism. But this is a complex task not least because space itself is a dynamic process between the ongoing historical geographies of territories (places, cities, regions, nations etc.) and the relational geographies constructed, for example, as the often only fleeting means through which circuits of value might take place. And, as indicated above, territorial and relational geographies are mutually formative. Place is complex and forever changing especially given the high dynamics – seconds are an increasingly significant measure of time in finance capital – of capitalist circuits of value.

However, whilst Harvey's critique of Williams' notion of militant particularism – "[T]he concept of 'place' that Williams evokes turns out to be much more complicated than he imagined" (2000: 57) – is spot on and profound, Harvey is also unwilling to consider that geography may be more formative than he imagines. And yet, Harvey's central concern for geography – "[We] have ... to recognize the geographical dimension and grounding for class struggle" (2000: 55) – underpins his long-standing concern to show "that there are ways to integrate spatialities into Marxist theory and practice without necessarily disrupting central propositions" (2000: 58). But this gets to crux of this debate around the significance of geography for Marxist theory and politics. Harvey's willingness to see geography as a powerfully formative force in class struggle but not to accept that geography might also begin to question and open up the 'central propositions' in a more fluid and open ended fashion – so implying that they are always and everywhere invariable – is problematic, inconsistent and unexplained. These lacunae open up the potential, at least, for a reconsideration of them.

Thus the argument which follows is that these 'central propositions' are not so foundational as to be fixed and permanent. Geography is too powerful a force for that. Indeed, it is precisely the dynamics and complexity of place and space that may lead to the questioning of such central propositions and so also question the notion that militant particularism should be dismissed as a potential 'space of hope'.

Whilst David Harvey (1996: 324) argues

"anti-capitalist movements form a potential basis for that 'militant particularism' that can acquire global ambition, left to themselves they are easily dominated by the power of capital to coordinate accumulation across universal but fragmented space. The potentiality for militant particularism, embedded in place runs the risk of sliding back into a parochialist politics ...",

Paul Routledge responds that "[u]niversal values are always embedded in, and emergent from, the local and concrete" (2003: 347). But the local and the concrete are never just that. In relational space, the reverse of this proposition is also true. Places (territories) are always in a process of formation from ever emergent relational geographies (of circuits of value, for example), just as they shape the emergence of such geographies. Thus local values may emerge from the universal. It is, then, not only the case that "ideals forged out of the affirmative experience of solidarities in one place have the potential to get generalized and universalized as a working model for a new form of society that will benefit all humanity" (Routledge 2003: 337), as universal working models may give rise to a diversity of new forms of society when subjected to the transformations associated with the mutual shaping of relational and territorial geographies.

One of the universal 'central propositions' to which Harvey refers is that of the predominance and determinative significance of capitalist social relations of value. If this notion of value is accepted unproblematically – and Gibson-Graham (2006) would argue that a capitalocentric view of the world induces such an unproblematic acceptance – then the risk of 'sliding back into a 'parochialist politics' is ever present as capitalism is always central and definitive. In contrast, the spaces of the ordinary economy (Lee 2006) enable the practice – often simultaneously – of different notions of value and, in this, they are transformative: capitalist social relations are always and forever limited. Indeed, the problem is less a 'sliding back' to capitalism/parochial politics form an economic geography of difference than the provision of further support for capitalism.

However, to paraphrase Susan Smith (2005: 17)

"... the politics and ethics of economic geographies can be challenged ... by making a bid for them; by embracing a thousand tiny ordinary economic geographies [in which notions of] value are not given but made ... the diversity of actually existing ordinary economic geographies and the multitude of normative ideas and practices that are, or could be built into them, is not just a new economic geography, or a social curiosity: it is a far-reaching political resource".

In this way – as Harvey (2001: 186) suggests –

"The return of theory to the world of daily political practices across a variegated and hierarchically structured geographical space of social and ecological variation can ... become both the aim and the reward of a particular kind of theoretical practice".

However, this is not so easy and begs the kinds of questions concerning the autonomy of diverse/alternative/other economic geographies raised earlier in this paper. As Dave Featherstone (1998: 24, 23) has pointed out, Harvey sets his argument up in such a way that it is impossible to enable such a return to 'daily political practices' in opposition to capitalism:

"Harvey ... cannot ... seem to imagine anything which can oppose it except a meta-socialism ingrained with its own iron mask of totality ... [and] ... seeks to prescribe how the struggle should evolve without really discussing or seeking to understand its own creative and organic evolution

Are, then, these quotidian practices merely celebrations of difference incommensurate with strategic economic-geographical essentialism? Or are they materially and socially sustainable, able to act as an effective and strategic mobilising force for wider and more profound change?

Featherstone (1998: 24) suggests that what is needed to engage productively with notions of militant particularism is "to imagine open ways of putting local-scale politics in tension with other scales in a way which creates spaces where identities and ideas can be squeezed through each other's pores". But the ordinary economy is neither global nor local but both: it concerns the values at play in the practices of circuits of value. In this sense it is an integral part of all forms and place of economic activity. And it is present and practised by all economic agents in all forms of economy. So, then, the question becomes can the power of the ordinary economy be used and its diversity/otherness generalised to enable coherent political mobilisation around multiple non-capitalist social relations and values?

TOWARDS SOME CONCLUSIONS (AND SOME OTHER FUTURES?)

Any answers to these questions can only be suggestive and tentative. The intent of this paper is simply to provide some discussion around such questions rather than to assert a definitive answer. Such would, in any case, be impossible given the open-ended way in which territorial and relational geographies interact to create new spaces – not only of accumulation but of hope as well.

Central to any discussion of economic geography must be the nature of value. That is, after all what circuits of value are about. And here arguments around the diversity of value in the ordinary economy may be helpful. Value is, it is argued,

"socially constructed through the formative intersection of values and the ... practice of Theories of Value ... Economic geographies are, therefore, never monistic ... [and] ... constantly interrupted by alternative conceptions of value and social relations of value ..." (Lee 2006: 427, 428).

In all economic geographies multiple notions of value operate at all times. Indeed, even in the most hard-headed practices of capitalism, a range of values (not least associated with cooperation, for example) are, in practice, essential to its sustainability. In consequence, the possibilities of diverse/alternative/other economic geographies are ever present – and ever practised – and their relevance and sense continuously demonstrated in the quotidian activities involved in circuits of value. In this way, "the notion of diversity is ... integral to a potentially transformative politics of economic life ..." (Lee 2006: 429). And this is precisely why financial markets are such critically important regulators in the survival of the current phase of capitalism and why the massive abuse of their power has so enraged those adversely affected by the ongoing financial crisis.

The issue then becomes that of the political consciousness of the reality and potential of social construction of alternative/diverse/other economic geographies. And here Harvey's critique of static and partial senses of place in the formulation of difference become centrally important. Without a well-developed notion of the dynamics of the territorial and relational construction of place and space, othering can all too easily become a negative and dismissive gesture. Rather than opening up possibilities, it closes them down and replaces a sense of generosity and an ability to think and act differently with acts of rejection. In this way, an openness to the different values that do and may shape economic geographies becomes closed off and the realisation of transformation becomes impossible.

Acknowledgement: This is a slightly revised version of a talk given at Katholische Universität Eichstätt-Ingolstadt on 25 January 2012. I am very grateful both to Hans-Martin Zademach and Sebastian Hillebrand for kindly giving me the opportunity to present this talk and to its audience for listening and for asking a series of questions which made me think very hard – if not so effectively.

Placing the Practices of Alternative Economic Geographies: Alternative Retail, the Spaces of Intention and Ethical Ambiguities

Michael K. Goodman and Raymond Bryant

INTRODUCTION

Many now take seriously sustainable and ethical consumption as well as its implications for how we understand contemporary spatial relations of consumer society and their bid in creating more sustainable lifestyles and alternative economic geographies (e.g. Barnett et al. 2011; Lewis and Potter 2011). In this, Barnett et al. (2005 25) have sought to fashion

"...an argument about the relationships between consumption, ethics and political action that starts from the assumption that there is no good reason to suppose that spatial distance necessarily diminishes either a felt responsibility or practical capacity to care for others".

For us, though, outside of the work of very few (e.g. Malpass et al. 2007), the complex role of place in constructing the material and discursive bases of ethical consumption tends to be glossed over. As we have argued elsewhere (Bryant and Goodman 2004; Goodman 2004), the deployment of place in transnational ethical consumption networks – notably in the 'imagineered' (Routledge 1997) descriptions of producer-based political ecologies – is fundamental to the connection-making relational ethics underpinning them[1]. Indeed, such deployment in the form of labelling schemes and provisioning figures greatly in the flourishing ethically-inflected local and regional food movements and economies in the UK and US (e.g. Eden et al. 2008; Morgan et al. 2006; Rangnekar and Wilkinson 2011; Selfa and Qazi 2005). Thus, the politics of 'caring at a distance' that Barnett et al. (2005) link to ethical consumption and its processes of working to create economic alterities is often only really realised in producer-consumer networks that encompass and blur place(s) through connections across the everyday spaces of what Lee (2006) calls the 'ordinary economy'.

More specifically, research and writing has barely just begun to explore in any real detail the fundamentally important 'place' of retail – and that particularly of 'alternative' retail – in the creation and practices of alternative economic geographies. Here, related work has focused more diffusely on 'political shopping' and 'political consumerism' (e.g. Clarke 2008; Clarke et al. 2007; Hawkins 2012a, b; Micheletti 2003; Sassatelli 2006; see also *Cultural Studies* 2008, Littler 2009 and Seyfang 2006a) which explores the politics of consumer choice and that of shopping practice in the contexts of more sustainable and ethical consumption. Others have developed a more specifically political economic focus into the ways that retailers control, shape, and 'discharge' – and so co-produce – alternative supply chains for more ethically-sourced goods such as organic and fair trade commodities (e.g. Barrientos and Dolan 2006; Freidberg 2003; Hughes 2005; Hughes et al. 2010). Some have explored the second-hand cultures of the charity

---

1 For alternative interpretations of the discourses embedded in ethical consumption fair trade networks, see Lyon (2006), Vural (2008), and Wright (2004); for the ways that celebrities are now involved in 'imagineering' and created spaces/places through development charity campaigns, see Goodman and Barnes (2011).

shop specifically (e.g. Gregson and Crewe 2003) where they analyse the 'shop-talk', shopping behaviours and wider material cultures of used 'things'[2]. Still others, and particularly Josée Johnston and her colleagues (Johnston 2008; Johnston and Szabo 2011; Johnston et al. 2009), have interrogated and critiqued the ways that alternative retail spaces and places – through in-store discourses, performativities and environments – work to produce corporate-enabled, 'consumer-citizen' hybrid subjectivities who are then encouraged to 'shop for change'; for Johnston et al., the place of alternative, albeit highly corporate, retail in the form of Whole Foods markets tends to dampen the possibilities of a more expansive and transformative food democracy given the limited and limiting consumer-oriented politics embedded in these forms of shopping for change.

In this chapter, we wish to build on Johnston et al.'s excellent and insightful work to more extensively explore the crucial role of the retail environment, discourses and performances – what we think of as the 'place of retail' and 'retail places' – in developing relationships amongst alternative retail spaces, consumers and their choices for more sustainable and ethical consumption; yet, unlike their work on what they call the 'corporate organic foodscape', we do this in the two specifically 'alternative' retail locations of the understudied charity and worldshops. Furthermore, we work to assess the ethical/moral characteristics of these relationalities and their potential ambiguities – given the drive for more consumption, but simply of a different kind, and co-incident globalisation of production/consumption networks – inherent in their material and discursive networks. Indeed, even so-called 'post-consumers' (Bryant and Brooks, forthcoming) need somewhere to shop and taking a first cut, as we do here, on two particular places of alternative retail and the sorts of (non)ambiguous ethics and behaviours they might create is one important and timely way to begin.

---

2   For recent work on the second-hand clothing trade more specifically, see Brooks (2012; 2013) and Brooks and Simon (2012).

This chapter builds on our wider project of assessing what we call the 'spaces of intention' (Bryant and Goodman forthcoming) that we see circulating, connecting and constructing ethical/sustainable consumption and production networks that enable alternative economic geographies to come into being through their practice. We perceive the spaces of intention containing the following elements.

- First, they involve epistemic collusions in that they involve a 'coming together' of ethically-enlivened knowledge claims, for example on climate change or social justice, that enable analytical and problem-solving sets of practices to be conceived and acted up in the first instance.
- Second, spaces of intention encompass reflexivity-in-action in that self- and otherly-awareness is heightened for debate but to also assign particular roles to the actors involved in the spaces of intention and their networked relationalities.
- Third, spaces of intention require affective orderings that work across and within difference and 'same-ness' to stitch together people and groups who have often never met and most likely will not do so. These affective orderings are often anchored in the emotions of care and responsibility that can act as the vectors to overcome and mediate social, economic, political and spatial differences and distances.
- Fourth, there are material and discursive place-making activities that 'people' the spaces of intention through the identification of specific populations through product marketing, regulatory regimes and the like, but also the 'placing' of space(s) through the identification of specific locations involved in – very often – the production and consumption of ethically-embedded commodities.
- Fifth and finally, we see the spaces of intention being tension-filled and politicised spaces that work to not only open up possibilities and so-called 'geographies of hope', but also those that 'bound', 'contain' and 'exclude' as much as they open up; one only has to think about the ways that fair trade or organic production standards

work at the local production level to both include but also exclude to get a sense of what we mean by this element (see Goodman et al. 2012, Mutersbaugh 2002, Wilson 2010).

Diffusely here then, the spaces of intention can, somewhat contentiously, be thought of as coming into being only through the drawing of borders and boundaries with some people, places and things excluded as well as others included; in essence certain opportunities are opened up for some people even as selected opportunities are closed down for other people in the spaces of intention.

What this chapter does, then, is explore the intermingling of space, place, and ethics in the constitution of a cultural economy of alternative retailing as a crucial and yet unexplored part of the spaces of intention that make up the practices of alternative economic geographies. It does so through comparative investigation of charity shops (specifically those of the NGO Oxfam), and worldshops (also labelled 'one-world shops'), i.e. independent stores located in the North that sell fair trade goods often produced in the South. The first concern here is to assess the role of Oxfam charity shops and worldshops as retail outlets that promote an 'expansive relational ethic' (Goodman 2004) that creates the intentional spaces of production and consumption in an alternative economy. Importantly, that role is seen to engender material and discursive ambiguities that complicate ethical appeals – especially for Oxfam shops.

The second concern is to explore the 'imagineering' of the ethically charged sense of place in these retail settings where used and/or fair trade goods are sold. Moral geographies are here created through a complex network of connections and disconnections among spaces and places of production, consumption, and retailing. This analysis then prompts a series of reflections designed to assess the broader import of alternative retail spaces. Here, the concern is to probe whether a 'retail of moral difference' can be discerned. By specifically taking Oxfam as one instance of charity retail, we explore how its shops are sites that are ripe with material and discursive ambiguity. In constructing an alternative, sustainable consumption place, Oxfam produces moralized discourses that infuse the practice of (re)selling items (including those once produced under dubious conditions) and the sale of fair trade products. Focussing on contradictions in such ethical fields, we consider how the fair trade slogan 'a better deal for producers' rubs up against Oxfam's implied notion of 'a better deal for the consumer' in the provisioning of brands sometimes produced with sweatshop labour.

Here, then, we contrast what we term a *second-hand ethics* of resell with a *first-hand ethics* of fair trade new-sell that define, at least in part, contemporary ethics in Oxfam shops. We further extend this analysis of ethical fields shaped by first- and second-hand ethics by examining previously little studied 'worldshops' – so named by the now defunct but influential Network of European Worldshops (NEWS)[3]. Selling only fair trade commodities, and instrumental today as a retail vehicle of the fair trade movement, we explore the first-hand moral economies and geographies created in this retail space. We also consider how the ethical field of the worldshop compares with that of Oxfam charity shops in constituting alternative retailing. Finally, the chapter concludes by suggesting that future research ought to consider in greater depth how complex ethical fields underpinning 'alternative' retailing may lead to new challenges and opportunities for the governance of the spaces of intention that make up alternative economic geographies.

While somewhat critical at times of Oxfam charity shops and worldshops, we nonetheless firmly salute their aim of making a difference by helping the poor through equitable exchange, notably between North and South, in the construction of more sustainable lifestyles. Still, such normative agreement must not blind us to the need to ex-

---

3   NEWS, along with International Fairtrade Association (IFAT) and the European Fairtrade Association, and with the support of the Fairtrade Organisations International (FLO), merged to form the World Fairtrade Organisation (WFTO) between 2008 and 2009.

plore ambiguities surrounding alternative retail, especially in today's neo-liberal commercial context. There is a critique here, then, of how the promotion of a commercial alternative can be compromised through material and discursive practices that simply legitimate the social value of consumerism (Mulligan 2007). And yet, when charity shops and worldshops are placed in wider social movement contexts, they might equally be seen to serve a useful 'propaganda' function for activists who need to demonstrate that 'there is an alternative' (however imperfect) to mainstream models promoted under neo-liberalism. Asking how charity and worldshops would construct moral geographies that differ from mainstream retailing is hence a fruitful place to start.

LOCATING ETHICS IN ALTERNATIVE RETAILING

Scholars who advocate a 'new retail geography' underline that exploring inter-related spaces of retailing and consumption means taking "cultural and economic geographies seriously" (Lowe 2002: 5). Much of this research emanating specifically from geography focuses on the UK charity shop, notably work by Gregson, Crewe, and Brooks. These scholars address the "connection between retailers and in-store geographies" in discourses of 'emplaced' talk and practice (Gregson et al. 2002a, 1663), ethnographies of shopping (Gregson et al. 2002b) and narratives of consumption and the body (Gregson et al. 2000). Such work, plus research on car-boot sales and 'retro-retailing', culminates in *second-hand cultures* (Gregson and Crewe 2003) where 'marginal' and alternative spaces of the charity shop are considered in detail. Here, a clear message to emerge from such work is that the meanings that people attach to the practices of 'alternative' and 'charity' shopping are decidedly ambiguous. As Goss (2004: 374) points out, Gregson et al.'s ethnographies reveal that charity-related consumption is less about moral economies of being 'alternative' and more about everyday activities that are "structured primarily by dominant discourses of thrift and value, or taste and distinction" (see also Gregson and Crewe 2003: 10-12).[4]

Allied work in retail management and non-profit studies also contributes to the ethnography of charity retail. The focus here is on evolving organisational and managerial traits of the charity shop qua business: the performance of volunteering (Parsons 2006), shop 'branding' (Girod 2005), the changing business climate (Horne 1998; Horne and Broadbridge 1995; Parsons 2002, 2004a) and 'professionalisation' of the workforce (Broadbridge and Parsons 2003, 2004; Parsons 2004b; Parsons and Broadbridge 2004). This research reveals how these traits generate ambiguity both in diverse day-to-day management operations and more widely with respect to the spread of upmarket goods (and hence prices) there.

If ethical concerns are not far from the surface in work on the shifting nature of how the 'charity business' (Lloyd 1993) works, there is a parallel interest in the ethics of what this sector produces in the way of items 'fit' for consumption. Here, that business can be seen to collide with the fair trade movement that is itself searching for new ways of getting across its products and message (Nichols 2002). True, the charity sector and the fair trade movement are both seeking to promote progressive moral geographies based on 'caring at a distance' (Smith 2000). Yet we suggest these institutions are nonetheless embedded in ethical fields shaped by ambiguity – a situation occasioned by their placement in a wider context where capitalist concerns are pre-eminent and actors are differentially empowered (Bryant 2005; Miller 2001; Sayer and Storper 1997; Smith 2000). Thus, to what extent and in what ways do alternative retailing (and consumption) practices mimic those in the mainstream sector? If they do, how far is an ethic of being 'al-

---

4   This is, however, an overly selective and essentialised reading of Gregson et al.'s work by Goss and hence fails to much more fully acknowledge the extent to which they do indeed address the – at least implied – ambiguities of 'alternativeness' in charity shops in their work.

ternative' eroded? How might complex ethical negotiations in alternative retail and consumption be understood?

To address such questions, we find it helpful to distinguish here between first-hand ethics and second-hand ethics in analysing alternative retail. First-hand ethics relates to the practice of selling (new) fair trade products and involves a holistic approach to production, sale and consumption based on normative rules of what is fair and equitable. This encompasses everything from transparent commodity chains to consumer education, from publication of codes of practice to direct cooperation with producers. In contrast, second-hand ethics relates to the practice of selling (typically) used donated goods and involves a disjointed approach to their production, sale and consumption. Here, there are no clear normative rules that unite production, sale and consumption – given that the alternative retailer does not control production. There is thus the potential for ethical vulnerability here as inconsistencies may arise between the ethics of production ('embedded' in the donations that are sold) and the ethics that the organisation may wish to promote in society generally.

On the one hand, then, there is the ethical field encompassing discourses and activities of the charity sector as a whole – geographies of care that inform each charity. Examples here include helping vulnerable children in the North (e.g. Bernardos), the poor of the South (e.g. Oxfam) or both (e.g. Save the Children). On the other hand, there is the sale in charity shops of ethically ambiguous clothes and toys, many produced under suspect labour and ecological conditions (Hale 2000; Hale and Shaw 2001; Klein 2000; see also Antipode 2004). While the sweat and bodily secretions of previous owners can be washed off clothes re-sold in charity shops (Gregson and Crewe 2003: 155-163; Gregson et al. 2000), it is much harder to wash out the permanent ethical 'imprint' of the sweated labour that was instrumental in the production of such commodities in the first place.

The situation is further complicated when we look at charity shops operated by Oxfam, one of the most successful charity 'brands' in the UK and beyond. Oxfam began life as the Oxford Committee for Famine Relief, a group initially dedicated to campaigning for food and medicine for civilians trapped in Greece during the Second World War. Subsequently, the organisation continued famine relief and poverty alleviation work, but has gone global working now in more than 70 countries around the world. It has also broadened the sorts of work that it does, as even a cursory glance through the Inside Oxfam magazine reveals. Thus, it is notably involved in political lobbying, consumer education, high street retailing, music festivals, general fundraising, disaster relief, community development, environmental conservation, and disease treatment. It has become a leading international NGO, recognised around the world with a powerful network of national organisations. In the UK, Oxfam's net income in 2011-12 was £282 million while charitable expenditure was £286 million, the difference made up through in-kind gifts and other income; its charity shops contributed around 8% of total income in that year, but was up £4 million from the previous year with increased donations of clothes and books. More than this, though, Oxfam's charity shops are the visible 'face' of the NGO in the UK with approximately more than 800 shops staffed by 22,000 volunteers. These shops constitute a vivid reminder of Oxfam's global fight against poverty and social injustice, including steps it takes to support alternative futures for the poor through fair trade.

Given this purpose, it is hardly surprising that, prominently displayed amongst the racks of donated items, can be found an array of fair trade goods. While no longer selling own-brand fair trade products, Oxfam does sell greeting cards from Global Crafts, soccer balls from the Play Fair Sports Company, Geobars from Traidcraft, and ubiquitous coffee, tea, and cocoa from Cafédirect (a company Oxfam helped to set up). That the first-hand ethics of fair trade sit side-by-side with the second-hand ethics of used goods is not lost on Oxfam. Indeed, in an early statement about ethical sourcing and purchasing (i.e. Oxfam 2007b), the organisation recognized that "[t]he globalisation of trade means that many of the goods on sale in the UK have been produced by people who experience dangerous or discriminatory working conditions."

How the places and spaces of production, consumption and charity play out in the discursive and material practices of Oxfam shops is treated further below.

Some of the ambiguities associated with first-hand and second-hand ethics can be seen when we contrast the ethical field of the Oxfam shop with that of the retail space of worldshops. Affiliated now with the WFTO, there are approximately some 3000 stores spread over many European countries that are exclusive retailers of fairly traded 'cultural products' (Littrell and Dickson 1999) such as crafts and textiles, as well as fair trade staples like coffee, chocolate, tea, nuts, and dried fruits. Worldshops also have a growing presence in the US and Canada through advocacy by the Mennonite fair trade organisation known as Ten Thousand Villages that has upwards of 180 stores. Overall, as NEWS (2007) put it already a few years ago, 'worldshops are the windows of Fair Trade to the wider world, influencing the choices people make as they do their everyday shopping'.

Worldshops have been wrongly overlooked as an important focus of study in their own right as increasingly significant players in alternative retailing. As with fair trade in general, they are dedicated spaces of intention seeking to connect consumers with producers across a host of commodities. Here, and building on Lowe's (2002: 6) aphorism that '[g]oods are substantiated through [retail] place and [retail] place makes consumption meaningful', we explore how worldshops attempt to distinguish themselves as ethically-based retail practices through exclusive provisioning of fair trade goods.

We now turn to an evaluation of the processes and ambiguities associated with first-hand and second-hand ethics manifested in the retailing practices of charity shops and worldshops.

TRANSPARENCY AND ETHICS IN CARING AT A DISTANCE

The moral geographies of Oxfam charity shops and worldshops reflect 'expansive relational ethics' (Goodman 2004). Both retailers promote the care of distant others: Oxfam through development work and fair trade sales, and worldshops through their exclusive stocking of fair trade items. Key here is transparency in retailing as well as copious amounts of consumer information. Yet how this process unfolds is another matter, as the two retailers reveal similarities and differences in practice.

Oxfam's ambiguous ethical fields

Walk through the door of any Oxfam charity shop and you are struck by the sheer amount of information provided to consumers. This variation on the 'network' and 'information' society (e.g. Castells 2000; Wittel 2001; Hughes 2000) constructs ethically-charged connections relating consumers to the world's poor through brochures, posters, product labels and sales tags. The production of transparent and useful knowledge is different, however, for used goods and fair trade goods. For the latter, there is an emphatic commitment to 'non-charity' and an associated crystal clear vision back along the commodity chain to producers and the political economy of production. For example, the Fairtrade Foundation's 2006 'Make Fairtrade Your Habit' campaign, not only let farmers and others speak for themselves but also provides vibrant images of (always) smiling producers engaged in fair trade practices. In another brochure, meanwhile, a 'bright future' is promised for people in the South who will be able 'to set up small businesses and work their way out of poverty'. A first-hand ethics comes shining through here in the attempt to connect places of production and consumption.

In contrast, used clothing (and other used items) for sale in these same shops reflects a second-hand ethics that prompts a different sort of representation by the organisation. Given that the fetish is intact in these items – production processes are hidden, after all, from consumers – Oxfam alters the direction and purpose of its moral lens. Here, the 'transparent' vision on offer is forward oriented – that is, towards distant and needy others who, it is stated, are the primary beneficiaries of money received as a result of consumer purchases. To this end, 'imagineered' sales tags are attached to many used items.

There are three things we need to note about these tags. First, they make the point that Oxfam is carefully targeting the kinds of people that it assists – the poorest of the poor. For example, the tag on one item of children's clothing proclaims: "£5.99 buys new clothes for a street kid in Ethiopia". There is a black and white photograph of six street children, smiling in new clothing presumably paid for out of funds generated in the shops. Second, the sales tags emphasise that Oxfam is carefully targeting the types of assistance it provides in order to maximise benefit to recipients. Thus, one tag suggests that "£7.99 buys cement to line a well in Mozambique", while "£1.99 helps to run a tree nursery in Bangladesh" – both practices vital to community welfare, as the accompanying photographs aim to illustrate. Third, the tags stress that Oxfam has 'global reach' in as much as it works with poor people around the world, albeit with a concentration in the poorest countries. The tags link assistance to specific places such as Mozambique, Ethiopia, Vietnam or Bangladesh – the better to underline the practical and tangible nature of this NGO's interventions.

In this way, consumers are invited to learn about and reflect on the plight of those less fortunate than themselves even as they are reminded that consumption in the shop is no ordinary exchange. Rather, it is an exchange (unlike in fair trade schemes) that is linked to forward-directed knowledge as to who benefits from Oxfam work – that is, of course, funded in part by the purchase of that well-worn (if 'hip') pair of jeans. Yet buying these items is simultaneously ordinary in that knowledge about the conditions of production remains sealed firmly from view, as with any conventional consumer product. As such, transparency backwards along the commodity chain is conspicuously absent – serving thereby to conveniently blot out ethically dubious product histories that might disrupt Oxfam's upbeat moral geographical imaginaries.

Here, then, in a shop in which both used and fair trade goods jostle for consumer attention, moral ambiguity is rife as the first-hand ethics of fair trade rub against the second-hand ethics of used goods. The ethical fields of Oxfam retailing are thereby blurred as they are interwoven. In the process, and given de facto product censorship surrounding used items rendered safely 'anonymous',[5] the majority of goods (which are indeed usually used) sold at Oxfam shops put a break on the expansive relational ethic of its operations. The sale of used goods in this manner enshrines a contradictory second-hand ethics at the heart of Oxfam retailing that simultaneously boosts income and ethical vulnerability – the latter relating to the charge of 'profiteering' from sweated labour.

The world(shop) of fair trade goods

Walk into a typical worldshop and, as with Oxfam, you are struck by the large amount of educational information available. Once again, there is careful imagineering: colourful and smiling images of distant Others in the guise of fair trade growers, weavers, and farmers dance before the eyes on products and posters, all of which are accompanied by livelihood stories. Yet there are points of contrast with Oxfam too as worldshops often mark themselves out through exotic scents (notably incense) – something that is very different from Oxfam shops

---

5   This is not to say, however, that consumers are immune to reflection on past use of items they purchase. See Gregson and Crewe (2003: 143) for a fascinating discussion of stories by consumers about former owners and uses of items that they have bought from charity shops. Still, such speculation about previous owners and consumers is different from 'deeper' knowledge about conditions faced by those who produced the items in the first place – which is our concern here.

where the smell of used goods (clothing, books, toys) is only partly camouflaged by the presence of 'sweet-smelling' fair trade items. Before considering in more detail the contrasting retail settings of worldshops and charity shops, we need to briefly present the history[6] and practices of worldshops.

Worldshops, fair trade and moral governance

While a cornerstone of the fair trade movement, the cultural economy of worldshops has received little attention. Indeed, even in-depth work on fair trade tends to focus on expansion into the mainstream, rather than on a dedicated fair trade retailer such as the worldshop (e.g. Low and Davenport 2005; Nicholls and Opal 2005; Raynolds et al. 2007). Such neglect obscures one of the more fascinating aspects of the fair trade movement. Self-billed as the "windows of Fair Trade" and one of the consumers' first points of contact with fair trade, worldshops are united in their function as a key site for promoting the fair trade model, even as they are differentiated by the manner in which they express that role. Thus, while all work to the same broad remit of selling and supporting fair trade, worldshops are nonetheless quite diverse, ranging from sophisticated high street outlets selling haute couture handbags from India to volunteer-run church back rooms selling basmati rice, medicinal teas, and Nepalese jewellery. At the same time, though, these diverse sites all sell fairly traded handicrafts – what Littrel and Dickson (1999) call 'cultural products' (see below).

Emerging from religiously inspired social movements that advocated a just international trading order in the 1970s and 1980s, and thereafter merging into the fair trade movement, worldshops are subject today to a series of governance regimes that purport to underpin the eth-

---

6   A full history including the role of worldshops in the contemporary fair trade movement has yet to be written, so this is only a partial and brief take.

ics of their retailing. Two interrelated regimes that construct, control and police are involved here. The first is that associated with the Fairtrade Labelling Organisations International (FLO) which regulates the circulation of fair trade goods in worldshops (but also fair trade goods in Oxfam shops); the FLO standards apply mainly to food commodities and once these commodities are certified as 'fair trade', they are festooned with the FLO logo.

The second certification/standards regime in worldshops is that developed and maintained by the WFTO, who, by contrast, assesses textiles and handicrafts. Here, rather than certifying individual products, it designates the groups and companies that sell these products through its 'WFTO Fair Trade Standard', thereby giving these institutions the cultural cache of 'WFTO' status. Worldshops, and the handicraft cooperatives and importers/exporters of these goods, must as the WFTO Code of Practice (2013) states, share the following practices of (1) a commitment to fair trade, (2) transparency in financial dealings and product sourcing, (3) ethical issues that focus on 'justice, employment, public accountability and progressive work practices', (4) safe and humane working conditions, (5) promoting equal employment opportunities, (6) the concern for people and quality of life and the natural world, (7) a concern for the environment, (8) a respect for producers' cultural identities, and (9) the promotion of fair trade by education and advocacy with consumers and the public.

These regimes define a first-hand ethics of fair trade, with worldshops as dedicated retailers of fair trade goods. Such regulation has an impact, not least in how 'good fair trade practice' is represented to consumers in these shops – thereby raising points of comparison with the situation faced by Oxfam shops.

Worldshop retailing: Visualizing production as 'non-charity'

The first-hand ethics of fair trade assumes storewide proportions in worldshops. From logos and slogans on products and posters to ubiquitous brochures near cash registers and store entrances, these shops present themselves as spaces wholly dedicated to educating consumers "to change consumption patterns based on issues of social justice and concern for the environment" (WFTO 2013). These materials, part of strategies Barnett et al. (2005: 31) argue govern ethical consumption more broadly, describe in detail the production and consumption of commodities for sale in worldshops. They thus help to make these spaces simultaneously ethical and political through carefully targeted knowledge dissemination. Further, and unlike ethical ambiguities noted with regard to Oxfam, worldshops seek to avoid ambiguity by only stocking fair trade goods, thereby conforming to the governance regimes described above. Hence, there is a distinctively comprehensive ethical vision about the production of all their goods that is noticeably lacking in Oxfam counterparts.

With nothing to hide, political 'shop talk' is encouraged at worldshops as part of a wider education campaign. Strategies include engaging consumers through questions and answers about fair trade, drawing attention to particular items and their ethical production, or generally serving as a meeting place for like-minded individuals who come to discuss, share ideas, and exchange views. Such talk is seemingly akin to that of the 'charity talk' that Gregson et al. (2002a, b) discuss. Yet there are important differences here too. At Oxfam, political talk is selective – comprehensive about some things (such as fair trade items and the forward-looking benefits of Oxfam development work made possible through shop purchases), but coy and evasive about other things (such as the production conditions of donated goods that may have been made with sweatshop labour). In the worldshop, in contrast, there is greater freedom to compare fair trade commodity chains (proclaimed to define production and consumption for all worldshop items) with unfair trade commodity chains (which shape production and consumption in mainstream commerce). Here, having nothing to hide means that these shops (unlike Oxfam shops) have nothing to lose. Indeed, they have everything to gain, as wide-ranging political talk helps to promote business in a retail world bedevilled by ambiguity.

These two retailers may also be compared on other matters. Consider, for instance, how worldshops are resolutely 'non-charity' in outlook. True, these shops vary a good deal among themselves – some more 'business-like', others more 'amateur' for example – as to how they operate. Yet, a core premise linking them is that they are not about charity in as much as they promote an alternative business model. 'Trade not aid' – the overarching and historical slogan of the whole fair trade movement since it began – works to develop "...relationships within a framework of solidarity, trust and mutual respect..." that "are based on reciprocal benefits and fair exchanges" designed to "achieve commercial efficiency at the least possible cost in order to open up markets to benefit producers" (WFTO 2013). Here, the mantra 'people before profits' becomes 'people and profits' – the better to support equitable economic relations between producers, retailers, and consumers in the marketplace. As with charity shops, then, retailing in worldshops reflects faith in the utility of the market, as well as a recognition that profit is essential to the process, albeit profit that is ploughed back into the organisation not to shareholders. Yet, whereas Oxfam shops are there notably to fund charity work, worldshops eschew charity altogether in favour of an alternative business model based on fair trade.

SPACES, PLACES AND CHARITY AND WORLDSHOP MORAL GEOGRAPHIES

Yet, in the case of both worldshops and Oxfam charity shops, issues surrounding the role of space and place in the construction of moral geographies of alternative retailing loom large. Here, recent work, notably by Barnett et al. (2005), considers inter-linkages of space and place thereby engaging with wider debates on these concepts in the context of ethical and sustainable consumption (e.g. Malpass et al. 2007) and questions of the 'responsibilities' of the global North (Lawson 2007; Massey 2004).

In assessing ethical consumption and fair trade, these scholars challenge accounts of space and place that treat them as opposites. As they put it – echoing work on 'distanciation' and 'displacement' in commodity geographies (e.g. Cook and Crang 1996; Crang 1996) – "[p]lace is understood to be the location of clear-cut ethical commitments, while space serves as a shorthand for abstract, alienated relations in which distance intervenes to complicate and extend the range of moral duties" (Barnett et al. 2005: 24). In contrast, their work on the fair trade NGO Traidcraft is designed to illustrate ethical 'devices' and 'performances' that overcome spatially linked indifference thus enabling a politics of care and responsibility at a distance that complements equivalent place-based politics.

Still, in making their arguments Barnett et al. (2005) tend to lose sight of the fundamental place of place – both material and discursive – in fair trade and its consumption networks[7]. In our view, these authors only relate half a story – especially when one considers moral geographies of worldshop and charity shop retailing. Thus, and pace Barnett et al. (2005), both shops work assiduously to foster ethical relations across space. On the one hand, there are ethical governance regimes of worldshops that underpin material and discursive 'outreach' in fair trade. On the other hand, there are the selective yet explicit forward-looking connections to poor 'Others' made in Oxfam charity shops. In each case, expansive ethical fields work to overcome discursive and material spatial blockages upon which conventional commodity systems thrive.

Yet in doing so discursive devices are used that 'rough up' (Cook and Crang 1996) products in these shops so as to connect places of consumption to places where 'deserving Others' live – be they places solely of production in the case of worldshops or places of production (for fair trade goods) and development (donated goods) in the case of

---

7   See also Bernstein and Campling (2006: 435) who wish to omit investigation of the semiotics of place from commodity geographies.

Oxfam charity shops. Take, for example, Cafédirect's fair trade 'Machu Picchu Mountain Special' coffee that is sold in both worldshops and Oxfam shops. This single-origin product is grown by the COCLA cooperative which is clearly placed on the Andean hillsides near (scenic) Machu Picchu itself – however ecologically problematic – before being moved long-distance across space to be once more placed and sold on the shelves of these alternative retailers – for instance at the 'One World Shop' located in a backroom of St. John's Church in Central London. There is too, as we have seen, the example of those 'imagineered' sales tags that seek to connect place of purchase to place of development.

Here, then, there is a process of re-placement going on that connects consumers, retailers, producers and development beneficiaries within 'alternative' retailing. Indeed, what these connections do is blur place and space in the creation of expansive ethical fields. Consumption, as sustainable consumption, is thus re-placed as it finds its rightful place in the worldshop commodity chain or the Oxfam shop 'charity-chain'. Thus, it is the imagineered connections of place at a number of scales – shop floor to coffee field, charity shop to development project site – that are instrumental in constructing the caring at a distance that is seen to occur in Barnett et al.'s (2005) ethical consumption networks. In short, it is precisely the connection of production and consumption places that imbues seemingly abstract and alienating spaces between people, economic processes, and local biophysical environments with ethical content, thereby creating moral geographies of alternative retailing.

Retailing moral difference

The analysis so far has considered the ways in which ethics and place are brought strategically into play in alternative retailing. Complex material and discursive dynamics were seen to be occurring, notably in relation to the articulation of complex ethical fields (based on first- and/or second-hand ethics) and multi-scale imagineered places. Such dynamics raise questions, in turn, about the broader importance of a possible retailing of moral difference. We note three points in this regard.

First, worldshops and charity shops are increasingly aiming to boost quality in the fair trade (and in Oxfam's case, also donated) goods they sell, thereby raising questions about the relationship between 'alternative' status and the social construction of taste in these outlets (cf. Goodman 2010). True, the push for quality is being pursued in the fair trade market as a whole, as this niche sector enters the mainstream economy thanks to big retailers (e.g. Nicholls 2002; Nicholls and Opal 2005). In the process, fair trade has fast become a household name (Goodman et al. 2012; Low and Davenport 2005). By quality, we certainly mean 'better' tasting and looking. Yet, there is much more at play here than that inasmuch as talk of quality is always about cultural differentiation (Bourdieu 1984). It also involves a politicised ethics encompassing such things as 'alternative' development in the South (for example via fair trade) as well as the sense of personal 'moral selving' afforded to consumers through purchase of these commodities (Barnett et al. 2005; Harrison et al. 2005). For Oxfam in particular, the push for quality is an especially complex endeavour given the simultaneous provision of new and used goods – necessitating a campaign mindful of both new (fair trade) goods suppliers on the one hand, and donors of used goods on the other hand. And yet, to ratchet up the 'quality' of the latter has become integral to its operations[8]. For example, the 'Sorted!' campaign specifically asked donors to sort through their donations so that only 'sellable' items would be passed on.

Oxfam's promotion of specialist-cum-designer goods and even shops has taken this quest for taste to new heights. Thus, there is the

---

8 There is here a wider story: even fiercer competition over low-end goods from cheap clothes retailers combines with increased competition within the charity sector (itself suffering from 'charity-fatigue') to make the need to try and go up-market quite imperative – even if only to stay in business (Broadbridge and Parsons 2003; Low and Davenport 2005; Parsons 2002).

Oxfam 'Originals' line of shops dedicated to selling retro and vintage fashion, as well as stand-alone book, furniture and music stores, and even dedicated bridal shops (with dresses up to £600 for designer gowns). Meanwhile, there is also the 'Valued' programme which sells high-end goods (such as antiques and paintings) and books on eBay, as well as the 'Unwrapped' programme which sells unusual gifts such as goats and alpacas for the South's poor. Indeed, the designer 'makeover' of Oxfam's clothing stock – aided and abetted by calls for donations that specifically include designer-label clothing – received an unprecedented boost from Victoria (Posh Spice) Beckham back in 2006 when she purchased a cocktail dress and fashion book from the Notting Hill Oxfam store. Thereafter, donations to that store soared by 70% even as customer visits trebled in number, giving rise to a 'Posh effect' in UK charity. All of this builds Oxfam's brand value as a leader in 'quality' provisioning as stated a few years ago:

"Do you have a flair for fashion? Are you passionate about clothes? With over 600 shops selling clothing, Oxfam can be relied upon to provide the perfect item at an affordable price. Whether you are searching for a designer dress, stylish suit or the ultimate accessory, Oxfam shops are the place to look. At Oxfam we aim to offer our customers a wide range of choice. We stock fashion for men and women, sportswear, outdoor clothing, shoes, fancy dress and much more. If you are looking for something unusual, please ask the shop team whether they have it in stock. All the clothing, shoes and accessories donated to our shops are carefully sorted to ensure you get good quality at a fair price. Our shops only sell items that we think our customers will want to buy." (Oxfam 2007a)

Secondly, there are differences in how Oxfam shops and world-shops go about pricing their goods reflective notably of differences in their sourcing. Thus, and its push for quality notwithstanding, most Oxfam stores still stock an array of goods sold at relatively cheap prices. Here, the fact of their reliance on used goods is to be noted – which means that most goods that enter their doors are virtually free to the NGO (there are small costs associated with sorting, pricing and transporting). Almost by definition, then, there is considerable profit to be made from the sale of these goods – a boon to the fortunes of a charity shop like Oxfam. That profit will depend on the prices that donated goods sell for – which is, in turn, linked to local high street market conditions and consumers' associated willingness-to-pay. In a number of cases and places, they are re-sold 'cheaply', especially where brand names are not involved and/or when stock needs to be turned over quickly (via price discounts and 'sales') to make space for newly arrived goods. In contrast, worldshops clearly do not enjoy the economic windfall that is donated goods. Instead, their goods have to be paid for – and at 'fair' (above conventional market) prices to producers at that. Hence, worldshops are not in the position that Oxfam shops are to be able to conduct alternative retailing 'on the cheap' – indeed, for worldshops to do so would even raise troubling questions about the way in which they were conducting business with fair trade producers.

In any event, worldshops are not cheap by design, as the idea is to generate as much added value as possible. Thus, difference is cultivated not only in a relative ability to pay for pricey goods, but also in what is provided in return: 'quality' foods and 'ethnic' handicrafts. While thoughtfully critiqued by Johnston (2002) and Varul (2008; see also Hendrickson 1996) as an objectification of the Other, our point here is rather that the aim of this pricing policy (excluding poorer consumers) is precisely to extract more money for 'caring at a distance'. A 'solidarity premium' is paid even as consumers are encouraged to develop a sense of ethically directed solidarity that celebrates difference (Goodman 2004). Here in the worldshop, then, is a call to solidarity that echoes, albeit in a different fashion, the one that was noted earlier in relation to Oxfam sales tags. Increasing the quality (and hence price) of fair trade products as a means to promote equitable development and respect for difference is thus a growing concern in worldshops. For example, Ten Thousand Villages (personal communication 2004) has re-designed goods in keeping with a fashionable fusion of Northern tastes and Southern 'traditional' styles in order to pique consumer interest. To this end, it employs style consultants to work with producers in order to enhance the quality of artisan products offered for sale to solidarity-seeking and premium-price-paying Northern consumers.

Third, the alternative retailers considered herein intersect with a growing society-wide concern to protect the biophysical environment, raising another facet to a possible retailing of moral difference. Yet, here, ambiguity and contradiction abound. Take, for instance, the first-hand ethics associated with selling fair trade goods in worldshops and Oxfam shops. Now, in purely environmental terms, such sales are decidedly ambiguous. On the one hand, fair trade goods are produced under conditions that may be broadly described as environmentally benign; foods are often (but not always) organic while handicrafts often rely on the re-use of materials and/or extraction from sustainable sources. Indeed, 'ecologically sound production' is included in fair trade criteria stipulated by WFTO. On the other hand, fair trade goods are coming under fire because they entail 'excessive' food/commodity miles reflective of a large carbon footprint[9]. Indeed, the very success of fair trade compounds this problem – raising uncomfortable questions about the broader ecological wisdom of this commercial form of caring at a distance (Averill 2007; Kelland 2007).

Here, the Oxfam charity shop may outshine the worldshop since used goods that it sells represent ecologically commendable 'recycled

---

9   Food miles are the number of miles a particular food commodity travels from field to fork, the reduction of which is now the cornerstone of local food movements (Born and Purcell 2006; Seyfang 2006). Part of this argument is the fact that the less miles travelled, the less resources used in transportation, and thus the smaller the total carbon footprint (the amount of carbon emitted to the atmosphere) contributing to climate change. Fair trade, with its need for international travel and larger carbon footprints than local trade, is coming under scrutiny from 'food miles' critics, although the discussion is now beginning to centre on the question of 'fair miles'; see, for example, the pioneering work of Macgregor and Vorley (2006).

consumption' – indeed, perhaps even a model for 'throw away' societies. This practice reduces the impact of consumption as shoppers substitute used for new goods, thereby giving discarded clothes, toys and
books a new lease of life. True, recycled consumption is still miniscule
when compared to overall consumption patterns. Yet, at least some
consumption has been re-routed in this way – in the process providing
partial relief to overburdened landfill sites. Given growing waste dis-
posal problems, the re-circulation of goods provides extra breathing
room for policymakers as they grapple with this crisis. It drags out an
otherwise rapid and damaging process (production, consumption, dis-
posal) that is the bane of modern capitalism (Redclift 1997; Royte
2005).

Yet this is no radical solution. Prolonging the consumption cycle
only postpones the outcome. It does not address a basic flaw in contemporary consumption-driven capitalism. Such re-circulation may
simply reinforce wasteful consumption, as charity shops help 'marginal' and/or bargain-hungry consumers to partake in a high consumption
lifestyle. As one Oxfam shop leaflet observes: "We always try to price
your donations attractively and fairly. Our customers often tell us:
'That's just what I've been looking for.' Sorted!"

CONCLUSION: ETHICAL AMBIGUITIES IN THE SPACES AND PRACTICES OF ALTERNATIVE ECONOMIC GEOGRAPHIES

This chapter has explored the mingling of space, place, and ethics in
cultural economies of alternative retailing with reference to Oxfam
charity shops and independent worldshops. It argued that material and
discursive ambiguities surround this endeavour complicating their
ethical appeal. This is especially so for Oxfam's shops where uncrit-
ical acceptance of donated goods has resulted in the propagation of a
second-hand ethics. In contrast, a strict focus on fair trade at
worldshops prompts a first-hand ethics where nasty conditions of orig-

inal production are banished. Yet, once an environmental dimension is added, that focus became the source of a new problem: a heavy carbon footprint (linked to transporting goods from the South to the North).

The chapter also examined some of the strategic choices that alternative retailers face. The 'imagineering' of ethically charged place in these outlets prompts complex moral geographies in which connections and disconnections between places of production, consumption, and retailing are selectively emphasised. Whether via 'forward looking' sales tags at Oxfam shops or fair trade foods and handicrafts at worldshops (also to some extent at Oxfam), material and discursive choices are made that are never innocent but rather are crafted to maximise an ethically-based 'alternative' consumption experience. Yet retailing moral difference prompts ambiguities over quality and price, value for consumers, and the environmental ramifications of that experience.

Indeed, one of the key points to emerge from this chapter is that considerable ambiguity surrounds the extent and meaning of 'alternative' retailing on the landscape of alternative economic geographies. Thus, as the environmental record of fair trade suggests, there may be a fundamental ethical contradiction at the heart of this process that will erode its appeal. Contradictions also abound, meanwhile, when alternative retailing rides on the coattails of mainstream relations of production and consumption as the Oxfam experience with donated goods sometimes produced under unethical conditions revealed. Thus, in scaling up from the everyday, micro-spaces of alternative retail to those of the complex and contentious environments of sustainability governance and policy, the ambiguities of the practices of more sustainable consumption – situated as they are in the contexts of neoliberal markets – must be front and centre. And, this involves not only understanding the retail places and spaces, which forms one of the key ways most 'post' consumers engage with sustainable consumption, but also the very ethical relations retail-scapes work to forge between shoppers, goods, and environmental and social justice.

In light of these findings, it is appropriate to suggest three ways in which future research could serve to clarify further the position of alternative retailing in the context of sustainable consumption and lifestyles. First of all, research is needed that examines the precise material and discursive relationships that link alternative retailing to other elements in the broader movements for sustainable lifestyles and not least, the ramifications of those links. Thus, how does such retailing – which asserts a retailing of moral difference even as it tends to use and hence legitimate many sales techniques and discourses found in the mainstream sector – fit with other strands in the cultural and economic promotion of an 'alternative' to the status quo? Much credence is given in alternative movements, for example, to the notion that 'transformed' means are as important as transformed ends – that how you pursue social justice is equally critical as attaining such an end. To what extent, though, does the rise of alternative retailing – indeed, the spread of sustainable consumption as political practice more generally (e.g. Jackson 2006; Princen et al. 2002) – subvert and/or promote this social movement maxim?

Secondly, and in particular, work is needed on the reciprocal nature of the relationship between alternative retailing and its much larger mainstream counterpart, especially in the context of 'planning' for and the governance of more sustainable consumption and production. We noted how the former is not always that different from the latter. This is perhaps not surprising given the ubiquity of mainstream retailing. Tried and tested practices are bound to rub off. However, to what extent can we speak of distinctive alternative retail practices and if so what are the key aspects that define them? Further, how might pursuit of a retailing of moral difference and sustainable consumption behaviours afford new opportunities to mainstream retailers? This is more than simply charting the spread of fair trade into supermarkets and the like. There is the bigger question here of how the essence of 'alternative' – encompassing process and product – may be used to boost the mainstream. As the boundary between 'alternative' and 'mainstream' becomes blurred, will alternative retailing even lose its political, economic and cultural utility?

Finally, what does the rise of alternative retailing in the pursuit of sustainable lifestyles as described here reveal about the future direction of a cultural politics of economic radicalism? Are there radical alternatives to it and if so, what are they, and more importantly, how do they avoid the pitfalls of cooption? Does the answer reside in a variant on the 'small is beautiful' argument coupled to small-scale non-capitalist exchange in LETS economies for instance (see, e.g. Lee et al. 2004)? Certainly, the growing environmental predicament might suggest this course of action. And yet, would this not simply be a collapse into a reactionary politics of the local – a politics with little or no place for caring about 'distant Others' (cf. DuPuis and Goodman 2005)? After all, part of the political attraction of alternative retailing (linked to fair trade) is precisely that it is a mechanism, however flawed, for tackling social injustice worldwide.

These are big questions that perhaps cannot ever be answered in a satisfactory manner. Yet, each in their own way points to the larger social and historical importance of the kinds of alternative retailing discussed in this chapter, as well as the possibility that the uneasy compromises and awkward ambiguities that bedevil such practices may be a small price to pay given the stark and often unpalatable features of the alternatives that can be imagined. The compromises of alternative retailing – and sustainable consumption more broadly – may thus, in the end, be a price worth paying.

Social Enterprise, Social Innovation and Alternative Economies: Insights from Fair Trade and Renewable Energy

Benjamin Huybrechts

INTRODUCTION

The transition towards a more sustainable economic system is increasingly seen as an urgency to respond to the social, environmental and economic challenges of our times. Mirroring this increased attention, the scholarly literature on transition and transition management, 'degrowth' and sustainable development (e.g. Loorbach 2007; Boulanger 2008) has considerably developed across a set of disciplines (sociology, geography, economics, engineering, etc.). The solutions put forth by the different literature streams vary to a large extent and rely on distinct if not opposed ideological foundations, from the radical, anti-consumerist vision of degrowth to the much softer and vaguer, reformist trend of sustainable development.

Common to the different literature streams, however, is to mainly focus on two levels of analysis. First, the systemic level receives most attention when it comes to diagnoses of limitations in the extant system and exploration of what alternative – non-growth, post-transition or at least sustainable – systems or economies would look like. This focus on systems is logical given the scope of the expected (r)evolutions to undertake. It is also coherent with the main disciplines involved in this 'macro-level' research effort: economics, sociology, political science, philosophy, etc.

A second and subsequent level of analysis that has been considered lies at the other extreme of the continuum: the individual. Indeed, as the failures of the extant economic system have been linked to the unrealistic and ideologically oriented vision of the individual as an ever-calculating, utility-maximizing "homo oeconomicus" (Stiglitz 2009), questions have arisen about the human behaviour required to generate or at least participate in the alternative systems conceived at the macro level. Put another way, to what extent and in what sense do we need to change our individual behaviours, in terms of purchasing, working, voting, investing, moving, and acting in general, in order to liberate ourselves from the homo oeconomicus patterns and consider alternative behaviours that, put together, may contribute to alternative systems? This 'micro-level' perspective has relied on work in psychology and anthropology in order to (re)discover new avenues for increased reflexivity and conscious action.

Between the macro and micro perspectives lie a diversity of 'meso' actors consisting of more or less formalized groups of individuals, organisations and institutions such as: public authorities (from local to global), businesses, civil society, educational institutions, etc. Much work has been undertaken on the role of these different types of 'meso-actor' in the transition towards alternative economies, but in view of the author of this chapter this has been developed either in a superficial way, mentioning the different actors to engage in these processes, or using 'black boxes' that suppose homogeneous sets of actors such as 'companies' or 'civil society actors'. In other words, although several case studies enter into the complexity of one or several of these black boxes, there is lack of clarity and depth in the study of how different types of actors, especially economic actors, may engage in and inspire societal change. In particular, little work makes the connection between how economic organisations function internally, and how they (may) act towards society (e.g. Moore et al. 2009).

This chapter does not aim, of course, to fill this knowledge gap on its own. It intends to bring a modest contribution to understanding the role of meso actors and in particular economic organisations by focusing on one specific, under-researched but important actor that is social enterprise. As will be described further, social enterprises are still weakly defined and heterogeneous (Dart 2004; Defourny and Nyssens 2010; Huybrechts and Nicholls 2012). Yet, they share two features that seem of particular interest in the debate mentioned here. First, they do not correspond to a neatly defined organisational category as they precisely lie at the intersection of two spheres that are commonly clearly separated and often opposed to each other: the market and the civil society. Such a 'hybrid' nature offers the potential for a specific and original contribution to the debate on alternative economies and systems, insofar as hybridity is synonym for innovation and unconventional thinking, as this chapter aims to show.

A second feature of social enterprises is their supposed coherence, at least theoretically, between internal functioning and external contribution. In other words, the new societal solutions that social enterprises offer through their products and services are supposed to be coherent with the solutions experimented within their very organisational structures. Despite their diversity and their obvious limitations, it is thus suggested here that examining social enterprises may offer at least two contributions to the discussion on alternative economies. First, by understanding the potential of hybridity, i.e. combination of distinct institutional patterns, to the reconfiguration of economic systems. Second, by highlighting the link between intra-organisational functioning and societal behaviour, in order to show how engaging actors in building alternative economies must involve in one way or another these two dimensions.

This chapter proceeds as follows. In the next section, the concept of 'social enterprise' is introduced and connected to that of 'social innovation', which can be seen at both the intra- and the extra-organisational levels. The features of social enterprises in dealing with social innovation, as highlighted in the conceptual discussion, are then illustrated in two areas: fair trade and renewable energy. After briefly presenting these fields in the third section, the fourth section explores the role and contributions of social enterprises in terms of social innovation and societal change based on the two fields. Finally, the conclusion summarizes and discusses the main elements of the analysis.

SOCIAL ENTERPRISE AND SOCIAL INNOVATION

The notions of social enterprise, social innovation and social entrepreneurship have received a growing attention over the last decades and have been used with diverse meanings and in a variety of contexts. Fair Trade, in particular, has been examined as a typical illustration of social enterprise (Doherty and Tranchell 2007; Huybrechts and Defourny 2008; Huybrechts 2012), social entrepreneurship (Nicholls 2006; Hervieux 2008) and social innovation (Mulgan et al. 2007; Phills et al. 2008). Although these terms set different boundaries around the observed phenomena and examine them under different perspectives, they are presented here, for the sake of clarity, as referring to different levels of analysis. Put simply, 'social entrepreneurship' would be the dynamic process through which specific types of individuals deserving the name of 'social entrepreneurs' create and develop organisations that may be defined as 'social enterprises' in order to experiment processes and/or generate outcomes defined as 'social innovation' (Mair and Marti 2006; Defourny and Nyssens 2008).

This chapter focuses on social enterprises as alternative organisational models capable of generating social innovations that can inspire and feed the transition of our societies. Two avenues for social innovation can be distinguished: 'external' and 'internal'. 'External' refers to the capacity of actors (here social enterprises) to engage in innovative solutions to unmet needs. 'Internal' refers to the innovative solutions experimented within the organisation. While these two avenues are conceptually distinct, they of course feed each other insofar innovations in organisation models may serve as experiments and drivers of new responses at the society level, as much as they should be reinforced by these new responses.

As the focus here lies on social enterprises as alternative and innovative organisation models, the most useful approach is based on the work developed by the EMES Network since the second half of the 1990s in Western Europe (Defourny 2001; Nyssens 2006). According to EMES, social enterprises can be defined as

"not-for-profit private organisations providing goods and services directly related to their explicit aim to benefit the community. They rely on a collective dynamics involving various types of stakeholders in their governing bodies, they place a high value on their autonomy and they bear economic risks linked to their activity" (Defourny and Nyssens 2008: 5).

These authors locate social enterprise within so-called third sector forms (non-profit or cooperative) that secure the pursuit of the social mission through a strong orientation towards a participatory management process as well as a democratic decision-making. In this sense, the EMES approach does not entirely subscribe to the idea of increasingly "blurred frontiers" among organisational forms, as suggested by other perspectives on social enterprise and social entrepreneurship (Dacin et al. 2010; Bacq and Janssen 2011; Nicholls and Murdock 2012).

In line with the participatory and democratic nature of social enterprise governance, the authors of the EMES network observe an increasing involvement of various stakeholders in the decision-making processes, leading to a 'multi-stakeholder' configuration. Such a configuration is associated with the variety of goals pursued by social enterprises – economic, social, and political – and the variety of resources raised (Petrella 2003; Campi et al. 2006; Defourny and Nyssens 2006). The insistence on the possibility of combining various types of resources – rather than on their sole market origin – contrasts with the approaches that focus on the market as the main or even exclusive source of resources. Finally, the EMES approach highlights the capacity of social innovation inherent in social enterprises through the different types of innovation distinguished by Schumpeter (Defourny 2001).

These social enterprise innovations are located at both an internal (new production processes) and an external level (new products and services, new market organisation, etc.). These levels can also be found in the broader literature on social innovation, where the latter is presented as both a process (new relationships within and around the organisation) and an outcome (new products and services). Whatever type of social innovation, most authors lay the emphasis on how the innovations are diffused across organisational and sector boundaries. Different diffusion steps can be distinguished, from prototypes and sustaining through building the organisational model, to external diffusion and ultimately systemic change.

This chapter proposes to examine the way in which social enterprises engage in social innovation and participate in alternative economies both internally and externally. Note that these two dimensions are not necessarily synonyms. While building alternatives to extant institutional arrangements necessarily requires innovative thinking, the reverse is not necessarily true. Indeed, innovations may be undertaken to better respond to social and environmental needs without seeking to contribute – at least potentially – to systemic change. The type of innovations that will be examined here, in the context of fair trade and renewable energy, are those that contribute to conceiving and experimenting intra- and inter-organisational arrangements and encompass the seeds of systemic change.

After the presentation of fair trade and renewable energies in the next section, the role of social enterprises in these fields will be examined and compared in terms of: (1) how they respond to unmet needs in society, (2) how their organisational models connect with their societal role, and (3) what inter-organisational strategies used to generate and diffuse social innovations at a societal level.

FAIR TRADE AND RENEWABLE ENERGY

Fair Trade

The origins of the Fair Trade (FT) movement are generally located just after the Second World War, with experimental initiatives of import and distribution of handicraft (e.g. Moore 2004; Nicholls and Opal 2005; Diaz Pedregal 2007; Raynolds et al. 2007). In the 1970s, the experimental fair trading partnerships were formalized into a model with explicit rules, and organisations were created specifically for this purpose. In the 1980s, several international networks were created to harmonize rules and practices, such as the International Federation for Alternative Trade[1] (Moore 2004; Diaz Pedregal 2007; Raynolds and Long 2007; Crowell and Reed 2009).

Labelling initiatives also appeared at that period, starting with "Max Havelaar" in the Netherlands. The various country-based labelling initiatives joined together into "Fairtrade Labeling Organisations International" (FLO or FLO-I), now "Fairtrade International", in 1997. The emergence of labelling has brought a fundamental change in the evolution of FT (Moore et al. 2006; Raynolds and Long 2007; Reed 2009). Indeed, it opened the door of the FT sector to any type of company through the possibility of having products recognized as meeting the FT standards by an external certifying body and not specific organisations. The participation of supermarkets and food multinationals in selling FT products resulted in a huge increase in the volume of FT sales but also in debates about the possible "dilution" of FT (Nicholls and Opal 2005; Moore et al. 2006; Raynolds and Wilkinson 2007; Jaffee 2010).

More recently, a range of new FT-focused businesses emerged, selling non-labelled FT products through both 'mainstream' and 'spe-

---

1 Later changed into 'International Fair Trade Association' and finally 'World Fair Trade Organization' in 2009.

cialized' outlets (such as worldshops). Although mainstream channels such as supermarkets now account for the largest part of the FT market, social enterprises still play an important role in producer support, education and advocacy, product development, new retail opportunities, and labelling and certification (Becchetti and Huybrechts 2008; Huybrechts 2012).

Renewable Energy

Over the last two decades, the field of renewable energy (RE) has tremendously developed, including wind and solar energy, but also hydropower, biomass and geothermal energy. RE sources (RES) have been increasingly promoted in the context of public climate policies aiming to reduce the dependency on non-renewable energies. In Europe, the '20-20-20' strategy aims to reduce carbon emissions by 20% and achieve 20% of RE by 2020.

Two main economic functions can be distinguished relating to RES: the production of RE and the supply of the produced energy, typically under the form of electricity based on RES ('E-RES'). According to the European Renewable Energy Council (EREC), the percentage of RES in the total production of energy in the EU has evolved from 8 to 12% between 2005 and 2010, and from 15 to 21% if we only consider electricity. The proportion of this energy produced by REScoops, however, remains weak although growing: from 1 or 2% in Southern and Eastern Europe, to 6% in Belgium and France and an estimate of 15% in Scandinavian countries (REScoop.eu 2011).

The market of energy supply, particularly in the form of electricity, is even more difficult to enter for REScoops, as it has only recently been liberalized and is still controlled by a small number of electrical companies. An additional difficulty is that the electricity grid is often owned by the historical electricity provider in each country. Several REScoops, however, have overcome these barriers and started distributing E-RES, with the goal of controlling a larger part of the supply chain and increasing their outreach towards customers and thus their membership.

In all countries, however, the RE market is dominated by large corporations. Although REScoops offer numerous advantages in terms of both economic efficiency and citizen involvement, they still represent a small share within the RE market (Huybrechts and Mertens 2011).

COMPARATIVE ANALYSIS

Responses to unmet needs

In both fields, social enterprises have been instrumental in conceiving new solutions to societal issues, thereby preparing concrete pathways for alternative economies. This is most evident in FT, where social enterprises have been pioneers in conceiving a whole, alternative system for trading with producers in the South. Based on diagnosis of the "unfairness" of international trade in terms of power asymmetries, unequal access to information and markets, unstable prices reflecting speculation rather than supply and demand etc., pioneers decided to move from campaigning and advocacy only, to concrete illustration of alternative ways of organizing the economic activity. This involved experimentations, negotiations, and creation of new networks across traditional sector boundaries (typically between NGOs and businesses). A number of key individuals such as priest Frans van der Hoff (Roozen and van der Hoff Boersma 2001; van der Hoff Boersma 2009) played an instrumental role throughout this process, not only as entrepreneurs, in the sense of creators of new organisations, but also more broadly as 'institutional entrepreneurs', creating new and alternative institutional arrangements and diffusing them at the system level (Maguire et al. 2004; Levy and Scully 2007).

New rules were set up to govern the trading relationships between marginalized producer groups in developing countries and importing organisations in the North, based on 'fair' and stable prices, partial pre-financing of the orderings, social premium for local projects, empowerment for producer groups, etc. These rules obviously responded to the needs of producer groups asking for better trading conditions and access to international markets. But the rules also responded to the aspirations of consumers for more ethical purchasing and, at least in the beginning, for (more) direct links with producers in the South (Goodman 2004; Nicholls and Opal 2005).

Indirectly, FT also answered the needs of other stakeholders concerned with the development of populations in the South, typically NGOs and governments (both South and North) having very little grasp on trading issues. In brief, it seems clear that FT was developed in response to a series of needs and aspirations that were clearly not met neither by the market nor by the state (Becchetti and Huybrechts 2008), as is often observed in the emergence of social enterprises (Defourny 2001; Santos 2012).

In RE, the first unmet needs that spring to mind are environmental ones. Clearly, dependence on fossil energies, evidence of climate change and technological innovations have brought needs and opportunities for developing RE facilities. These needs have been accentuated in recent years. In this case, many actors other than social enterprise were at the basis of the development of RE, including universities and research centres, governments, SMEs and large corporations. Nevertheless, the role and potential of social enterprises as alternative organisation models appears more clearly when examining the 'non-environmental' societal needs related to RE and energy in general. These needs and issues include, for instance, access to energy, citizen participation and local anchoring, transparency for customers, distribution of profits, and broader challenges of the ecological transition (reduction of energy consumption and building of a 'post-oil' society).

It is related to these different issues that social innovations were set up, not so much on the products itself (RE facilities are technological rather than social innovations), but more on the processes regarding the ownership, governance and objectives of RE production and/or supply. These process innovations include involvement of citizens in decision-making or even ownership of local 'short circuit' RE projects, reinvestment of profits into the local community, new types of alliances between energy businesses, local communities and public authorities, innovative schemes enabling poor households to consume from and own RE facilities, follow-up of citizens' energy consumption reductions, etc.

The innovations have been set up by environmental NGOs, local non-profit organisations, municipalities and, increasingly, social enterprises. Indeed, one answer to the abovementioned issues is when citizens come together to build community-owned businesses pursuing social and environmental aims prior to profit maximisation, i.e. REScoops.

Organisational models

In both sectors, social enterprises have not only been at the forefront of 'external' innovations through new solutions to societal problems; they have also tried to build internal organisational arrangements that are coherent with their societal goals and contrast with mainstream business practices.

In FT social enterprises, these internal arrangements can easily be compared with the requirements applying to the trading partnerships and particularly to producer groups. Typically, the requirement of democratic organisation and decision-making, applying until recently to producer groups in the FT system, was relatively taken-for-granted among pioneer social enterprises. The latter emerged as non-profit organisations and later cooperatives for which democratic decision-making in the governance structures (such as the general assembly) was legally statutory but also ideologically favoured (Huybrechts 2007; Becchetti and Huybrechts 2008).

One may question the 'innovative' character of democratic governance structures, as organisation forms such as the cooperative have existed for more than 150 years. But social innovation, however, does not necessarily imply new in the sense of 'never seen before', but rather new as 'contrasting with extant practices'. Many social innovations thus involve re-actualisation or adaptating 'old' devices in order to respond differently to societal challenges. Democratic decision-making along the supply chain, as experienced by FT social enterprises in the North and in the South, is one such example.

Another key governance issue is stakeholder participation, i.e. the way in which stakeholders not initially or formally members of the organisation are involved in the making and implementation of strategic decisions. In the FT system, producer groups have thus been encouraged to involve 'non-members' intervening in the production such as male producers' wives, cooperative staff and producers' temporary workers, etc. This has been mirrored to various extents in FT social enterprises in the North, many of which have associated their staff, partner NGOs, or consumer representatives in their decision-making. Going even further, some major FT importers have associated the producers groups with whom they interact through different schemes such as participation in the capital and/or representation on the board of directors (Davies et al. 2010; Huybrechts 2012). This has clearly reinforced the 'general interest' dimension of FT, with the aim of benefitting not only trading partners but also broader communities.

Case study: Divine Chocolate – Divine Chocolate is a FT social enterprise that was set up in 1998 through a partnership between Twin Trading (another FT social enterprise), The Body Shop Plc, and two charities (Comic Relief and Christian Aid). The social enterprise has focused on importing and distributing chocolate products through both alternative outlets (FT shops) and mainstream retailers. This has resulted in rapid growth and important benefits for small-scale cocoa farmers in West Africa. As for other FT social enterprises, the business activity is a means to support the social mission, i.e. to improve the livelihoods and opportunities for small-scale producers.

Interestingly, the social enterprise has sought to align its internal management and governance on its external social mission. This has resulted in an innovative governance scheme involving different stakeholders concerned by, and able to monitor, the pursuit of the economic activity explicitly directed towards the pursuit of the social mission. As the most concerned stakeholder, the cooperative of cocoa farmers 'Kuapa Kokoo' in Ghana has been more than just 'involved' as it has been given 45% ownership and has two seats on the Board of directors. This means that the producer organisation does not merely benefit from but can concretely shape and implement Divine's social mission. This pioneering mechanism in the FT and more broadly social enterprise sector allows producers "to gain added value from the entire value network and not just from the selling of the primary commodity" (Doherty 2011: 370). The governance structure also involves other key stakeholders such as founding and partner social enterprises (Twin Trading) and alternative financial institutions (Oikocredit). Divine has also developed strong connections with supporter networks in schools, universities and churches, and FT shops, which strongly contributes to its advocacy work.

In brief, Divine has been particularly innovative and pioneering not only in its work as a FT social enterprise but also in the alignment and consistency between social mission and internal governance structure, striving for "fairness" throughout the supply chain. The innovative governance of Divine has served as an example for many other FT social enterprises that are now implementing similar devices.

Such governance innovations can also be found in REScoops. While democratic decision-making has been a key feature of the cooperative model, participation has clearly not been a distinguishing feature historically. Indeed, as for-profit businesses, cooperatives primarily aimed to serve their members and were thus governed in a way that shares power among members only, consisting of one particular category such as consumers, producers or workers (Birchall 1997). Integrating a more general trend among cooperatives (Münkner 2004), REScoops have been conceived as 'multi-stakeholder' organisations in which different stakeholder groups intervene and in which different economic roles are combined by a same group of people – typically citizens who are also investors (through their shares in the coop), (co-)producers of energy, and consumers of this energy (Huybrechts and Mertens 2011).

Case study: Ecopower – Ecopower is a Belgian REScoop that was created in the 1990s from a student environmental protest organisation. The cooperative has built an impressive experience in setting up, managing and funding citizen-based RE projects, including wind turbines, small hydraulic projects, solar panels, and biomass. In the early 2000s, Ecopower obtained access to the grid in order to directly supply consumers all over Flanders. This dramatically increased the number of members (now exceeding 40,000) and the market position – Ecopower now supplies 1.1% of households in Flanders with green energy.

Consumers are all members who receive equal vote in the General Assembly. The cooperative seeks to educate its members in terms of rational energy use and ecological transition in general. This has resulted in an impressive decrease in the members' consumption (average of 30% over the first year of membership). Due to the profitability of RE projects, the cooperative has generated profits, but these have been mainly reinvested in the project but also in other REScoops across Europe. The founders wish to take advantage of their success to support growing citizen-based RE initiatives as well as other cooperatives, thereby contributing to cooperative relationships among cooperatives. To help diffuse citizen engagement in RE development and public appropriation of RE sources as 'public goods' (wind, sun, etc.), Ecopower has been instrumental in creating and sustaining networks at the national and international level (REScoop.be and REScoop.eu).

Innovative governance schemes have also been conceived to enable different levels of financial participation. Indeed, most REScoops have gained financial participation by a broad array of constituents, some of which directly concerned as inhabitants of the region of the RE facilities, others supporting the initiative as institutions, and still others more remote and with a more indirect stake. Different groups of cooperative members have thus been created to involve only relevant members to certain decisions and to avoid take-over by members with a less direct stake – in other words, to remain locally focused in spite of non-local participation. Another organisational innovation is the access to membership facilitated for poor households not able to afford one share. In some REScoops, shares have been given as a 'loan' reimburseable thanks to the future economies on energy consumption and in some cases on energy prices (see www.rescoop.eu for an overview of these innovative practices).

Diffusion strategies

Finally, it is suggested here that the diffusion of both internal and external social innovations as 'alternatives' to dominant models requires strategies that are partly similar to but also partly different from traditional innovations. The focus will be laid in this section on the specific features of social innovation diffusion. Two aspects are common to FT and REScoops: the open dimension of the diffusion process, and its connection with institutional change at the society level.

Both in the FT and REScoops case, the initial experimentations and gradual formalisation of the 'alternative' initiatives have been based on collective learning and information sharing. In FT, besides the joint structuring of rules through certification by labelling initiatives, extensive work has been devoted to developing networks enabling not only common representation of the movement's interests, but also exchange and sharing practices. These practices included identification of and information about producer groups, division of labour in terms of shipping and import, joint sales outlets, as well as joint education and advocacy initiatives (formalized into the creation of a common lobbying platform at the European level). In REScoops, the emphasis was laid from the beginning on replicating citizen groups and supporting them in setting up their cooperative. Due to the local and participative ambition of REScoops, the extension of the model has not consisted in having individual REScoops grow and become large, possibly multinational businesses, but rather in replicating REScoops in a large number of local contexts. In this process, pioneer successful REScoops have invested more than what their economic interest would allow in supporting new initiatives and help them grow and acquire legitimacy in their respective contexts. Similar supporting mechanisms have been observed in FT.

While some of the sharing and diffusion practices can be observed in other industries, specific in both cases presented here is the "openness" of information and practice sharing, as well as the collective endeavour of societal change in which such sharing takes place. Indeed, the goals of FT and citizen-owned RE, as genuine or potential social movements supported by networks of social enterprises and activists, extends far beyond the promotion of an industry to aim a more or less important societal change (according to the position on the continuum between 'reformist' and 'revolutionary' stances). This is consistent with the characterisation of social innovation diffusion, the ultimate step of which is 'systemic change', i.e. changes in behaviours, practices and rules at the global level that make the innovations "irreversible" (Callon 1986).

To achieve systemic change, what none of the alternatives examined here have achieved so far, it seems clear that broad and solid alliances are required. In both cases, alliances have been developed not only with other social movement and civil society actors, but also with public authorities and committed businesses. FT has featured innovative and successful multi-stakeholder collaborations such as the 'Fairtrade Towns' campaign (and its sisters of Fairtrade schools, churches, regions and even nations) or the 'Fairtrade@Work' program. REScoops have fewer records in this area but have started to engage in collaborations with transition networks, with municipalities and regions and with businesses, both at the local and at the global levels.

Case study: Fairtrade Towns – The Fairtade Town campaign emerged from the pioneering initiative of a local Oxfam group in the British town Garstang. The initiative aimed to promote Fair Trade at the local level by involving stakeholders such as the municipality, local charities and citizen groups, local businesses, schools, etc. Thanks to a large success and support by the Fairtrade Foundation, this scheme was replicated all over the UK. The principles for 'Fairtrade Town' certification were structured into five goals clearly extending the focus on FT to include broader sustainable development initiatives: explicit support from the council; availability of FT products in local shops and cafés; preference for FT in the consumption by local businesses and organisations; media coverage and stimulation of public support; and steering group involving representatives from different stakeholder categories.

The campaign was later replicated in many other countries and a FT town network was created with the support of the European Union. This campaign has successfully managed to gather diverse stakeholders, many of which not initial FT supports, around a local and stimulating project. Even if such a mobilisation of diverse actors may have diluted the 'alternative' dimension of FT and its political content, this case shows how a social innovation can be diffused precisely through innovative networking processes transforming passive stakeholders into active supporters.

Nevertheless, both initiatives inevitably face the same paradox when considering the diffusion of alternatives and the pursuit of systematic change. Indeed, as systemic change requires involving a broad array of partners, some of which are inevitably less 'alternative' and have interests in maintaining extant institutional arrangements, each further diffusion step comprises both the potential of deeper change and the risks of instrumentalisation and denaturation of the intended change (Hargrave and Van De Ven 2006). Hence, choices have to be made on who to involve and how in order to better serve the social enterprise systemic goals but also their economic needs. The different responses to these choices explain the divergences and possible conflicts among participants in the social innovation, as the evolution of the FT movement, divided into different branches, has shown.

CONCLUSION

This chapter has examined the role of social enterprises as alternative and innovative organisational models. Using the cases of Fair Trade and renewable energy, social enterprises have been shown to engage in innovative and potentially alternative action in three ways: (1) as pioneers in developing new goods and services responding to societal needs; (2) as pioneers in conceiving organisational models contrasting with those of traditional businesses and NGOs partly by hybridizing features from these established models; and (3) as creators and leaders of networks devoted to pursuing systemic change.

The cases of Fair Trade and REScoops demonstrate the potential of social enterprises in preparing and promoting alternative economies. But the cases have also shown the pitfalls of these hybrid models combining alternative ways of doing with integration in the extant economic landscape. This inevitably brings paradoxes for social enterprises that become located "in and against the market" (Le Velly 2004). Such paradox shows that social enterprises cannot imagine, build and sustain alternative economies alone; there place is of another type, that could be labelled "bridging" (Tracey et al. 2011). Indeed, because of their hybrid nature and their combination of social, economic and political goals, social enterprises connect different types of stakeholders, some of which are at the forefront of alternative thinking and action while others act within extant economic structures. Hence, social enterprises should not be seen as "solutions" on their own but rather as laboratories of alternative economic practices and as one among other pillars on which alternative economies can be conceived and built.

References

Aldridge, T. and Patterson, A. (2002): LETS get real: constraints on the development of Local Exchange Trading Schemes, in: Area 34(4), pp. 370-381.

Amin, A., Cameron, A. and Hudson, R. (2003): The Alterity of the Social Economy, in: A. Leyshon, R. Lee and C. Williams (eds.), Alternative Economic Spaces, London: Sage, pp. 27-54.

Antipode (2004): Intervention symposium: Geographies of anti-sweatshop activism, in: Antipode 36(2), pp. 191-226.

Audretsch, D. and Elston, J. (1997): Financing the German Mittelstand, Small Business Economics 9(2), pp. 97-110.

Averill, V. (2007): African trade fears carbon footprint backlash, in: BBC News, 21. February, available at: news.bbc.co.uk/1/hi/business/6383687.stm [first accessed October 2012].

Bacq, S. and Janssen, F. (2011): The multiple faces of social entrepreneurship: A review of definitional issues based on geographical and thematic criteria, in: Entrepreneurship & Regional Development: An International Journal 23, pp. 373-403.

Baimbridge, M., Birkitt, B., and Whyman, P. (eds.) (2006): Implications of the Euro: A critical perspective from the left, London: Routledge.

Barnett, C., Cloke, P., Clarke, N. and Malpass, A. (2005): Consuming ethics: Articulating the subjects and spaces of ethical consumption, in: Antipode 37(1), pp. 23-45.

Barnett, C., Cloke, P., Clarke, N. and Malpass, A. (2011): Globalizing responsibility: The political rationalities of ethical consumption, London: Blackwell.

Barrientos, S. and Dolan, C. (eds.) (2006): Ethical sourcing in the global food system. London: Earthscan.

Beccheti, L. and Hybrechts, B. (2008): The Dynamics of Fair Trade as a Mixed-form Market, in: Journal of Business Ethics 81, pp. 733-750.

Bernstein, H. and Campling, L. (2006): Review essay: Commodity studies and commodity fetishism ii: 'Profits with principles'?, in: Journal of Agrarian Change 6(3), pp. 414-447.

Berthoud, R. and Hinton, T. (1989): Credit Unions in the United Kingdom, London: Policy Studies Institute.

Birchall, J. (1997): The International Cooperative Movement, Manchester: Manchester University Press.

Boddy, M. and Fudge, C. (eds.) (1984): Local Socialism, London: Macmillan.

Bode, S. (2004): Potentiale regionaler Komplementärwährungen zur Förderung einer endogenen Regionalentwicklung, Osnabrück: Universität Osnabrück.

Bode, S. (2005): Regionale Währungen für entwicklungsschwache Regionen: Möglichkeiten für eine regionale Ökonomie, in: Zeitschrift für Sozialökonomie 42(144), pp. 3-10.

Bonefield, W. and Holloway, J. (eds.) (1996): Global Capital, National State and the Politics of Money, London: Macmillan.

Boulanger, P.M. (2008): Une gouvernance du changement sociétal: le transition management in: La Revue Nouvelle 11, pp. 61-73.

Broadridge, A. and Parsons, E. (2004): Gender and career choice: Experiences of UK charity retail managers, in: Career Development International 10(2), pp. 80-97.

Broadridge, A. and Parsons, L. (2003): Still serving the community? The professionalisation of the UK charity retail sector, in: International Journal of Retail & Distribution Management 31(8), 418-427.

Brooks, A. (2012): Riches from rags or persistent poverty? The working lives of second-hand clothing vendors in maputo, mozambique, in: Textile: The Journal of Cloth and Culture 10(2), pp. 222-237.

Brooks, A. (2013): Stretching global production networks: The international second-hand clothing trade, in: Geoforum 44(1), pp. 10-22.

Brooks, A. and Bryant, R. (forthcoming): Consumption, in: C. Death (ed.), Critical environmental politics, London: Routledge.

Brooks, A. and Simon, D. (2012): Untangling the relationship between used clothing imports and the decline of African clothing industries, in: Development and Change 43(6), pp. 1265-1290.

Bryant, R. (2005): Nongovernmental organizations in environmental struggles: Politics and the making of moral capital in the philippines, New Haven: Yale University Press.

Bryant, R. and Goodman, M. (2004): Consuming narratives: The political ecology of 'alternative' consumption, in: Transactions of the Institute of British Geographers 29(3), pp. 344-366.

Bryant, R. and Goodman, M. (forthcoming): Peopling the practices of sustainable consumption: Eco-chic and the limits to the spaces of intention, in: B. Barendregt and R. Jaffe (eds.), Green consumption: The global rise of eco-chic, London: Berg.

Callon, M. (1986): Some Elements of a Sociology of Translation: Domestication of the Scallops and the Fishermen of St Brieuc Bay in: J. Law (ed.), Power, Action and Belief: A New Sociology of Knowledge, London: Routledge, pp. 196-223.

Campi, S., Defourny, J. and Grégoire, O. (2006): Work integration social enterprises: are they multiple-goal and multi-stakeholder organizations?, in: M. Nyssens (ed.), Social Enterprise. At the crossroads of market, public policies and civil society, London: Routledge, pp. 29-49.

Castells, M. (2000): Materials for an exploratory theory of the network society in: British Journal of Sociology 51(1), pp. 5-24.

Cavanagh, J. and Mander, J. (2004): Alternatives to Economic Globalization, San Francisco: Berrett-Koehler Publishers.

CEC (Community Economies Collective) (2001): Imagining and Enacting Noncapitalist Futures, in: Socialist Review 28(3/4), pp. 93-135.

Chang, H.-J. (2007): Bad Samaritans: the guilty secrets of rich nations and the threat to global prosperity, London: Random House Business Books.

Clarke, N. (2008): From ethical consumerism to political consumption, in: Geography Compass 2(6), pp. 1870-1884.

Clarke, N., Barnett, C., Cloke, P. and Malpass, A. (2007): Globalising the consumer: Doing politics in an ethical register, in: Political Geography 26(3), pp. 231-249.

Conaty, P. and Mayo, E. (1997): A Commitment to People and Place: The Case for Community Development Credit Unions. Report for the National Consumer Council, London: New Economics Foundation.

Cook, I. and Crang, P. (1996): The world on a plate: Culinary culture, displacement, and geographical knowledges, in: Journal of Material Culture 1(2), pp. 131-153.

Cox, K.R. (2012): Marxism, Space and the Urban Question, in: A.E.G. Jonas and A. Wood (eds.), Territory, the State and Urban Politics, Farnham: Ashgate, pp. 55-75.

Crang, P. (1996): Displacement, consumption, and identity, in: Environment and Planning A 28(1), pp. 47-67.

Cripps, F., Griffith, J., Morrell, F., Reid, J., Townsend, P. and Weir, S. (1981): Manifesto: A Radical Stretegy for Britain's Future, London: Pan Politics.

Crowell, E. and Reed, D. (2009): Fair Trade: A Model for International Co-operation Among Co-operatives?, in: D. Reed and J.J. McMurtry (eds.), Co-operatives in a Global Economy: The Challenges of Co-operation Across Borders, Newcastle upon Tyne: Cambridge Scholars Publishing, pp. 141-177.

Cultural Studies (2008): Cultural studies and anti-consumerism: A critical encounter, in: Cultural Studies 22(5).

Dacin, P.A., Dacin, M.T. and Matear, M. (2010): Social Entrepreneurship: Why We Don't Need a New Theory and How We Move Forward From Here, in: Academy of Management Perspectives 24, pp. 37-57.

Dart, R. (2004): The legitimacy of social enterprise, in: Nonprofit Management & Leadership 14, pp. 411-424.

Dauncey, G. (1988): Beyond the crash: the emerging rainbow economy, London: Greenprint.

Davies, I., Doherty, B. and Knox, S. (2010): The Rise and Stall of a Fair Trade Pioneer: The Cafédirect Story, in: Journal of Business Ethics 92, pp. 127-147.

Daya, S. and Authar, R. (2012): Self, Others and Objects in an 'Alternative Economy': Personal Narratives from the Heiveld Rooibos Cooperative, in: Geoforum 43(5), pp. 885-893.

Defourny, J. (2001): From Third Sector to Social Enterprise, in: C. Borzaga and J. Defourny (eds.), The Emergence of Social Enterprise, London: Routledge.

Defourny, J. and Nyssens, M. (2006): Defining social enterprise, in: M. Nyssens (ed.), Social Enterprise. At the crossroads of market, public policies and civil society, London: Routledge, pp. 3-26.

Defourny, J. and Nyssens, M. (2008): Social Enterprise in Europe: Recent Trends and Developments, EMES Working Paper 08.

Defourny, J. and Nyssens, M. (2010): Conceptions of Social Enterprise and Social Entrepreneurship in Europe and the United States: Convergences and Divergences, in: Journal of Social Entrepreneurship 1(1), pp. 32-53.

DeGrauwe, P. (2000): Economics of Monetary Union, Oxford: Oxford University Press.

Diaz Pedegal, V. (2007): Le commerce équitable dans la France contemporaine. Idéologies et pratiques, Paris: L'Harmattan.

Dicken, P. (2011): Global shift, London: Sage.

Dinerstein, A. (2001): Roadblocks in Argentina: Against the violence of stability, in: Capital and Class 74, pp. 1-7.

Doherty, B. (2011): Resource advantage theory and fair trade social enterprises, in: Journal of Strategic Marketing 19, pp. 357-380.

Doherty, B. and Tranchell, S. (2007): 'Radical mainstreaming' of fairtrade: the case of The Day Chocolate Company, in: Equal Opportunities International 26, pp. 693-711.

Donadio, R. (2011): Battered by Economic Crisis, Greeks turn to Barter Networks, in: The New York Times, 1. October, available at: www.nytimes.com/2011/10/02/world/europe/in-greece-barter-networks-surge.html?pagewanted=all&_r=0 [first accessed October 2011].

Douthwaite, R. (1996): Short Circuit: Strengthening local economies for security in an uncertain world, Totnes, Devon: Green Books.

DuPuis, E.M. and Goodman, D. (2005): Should we go "home" to eat?: toward a reflexive politics of localism, in: Journal of Rural Studies 21(3), pp. 359-371.

Eden, S., Bear, C. and Walker, G. (2008): Mucky carrots and other proxies: Problematising the knowledge-fix for sustainable and ethical consumption, in: Geoforum 39(2), pp. 1044-1057.

Engel, A. (2010): Desire for/within Economic Transformation, in: e-flux journal 17, available at: www.e-flux.com/journal/desire-for-within-economic-transformation [first accessed December 2012].

Engels, F. (1892/1968): Socialism: Utopian and Scientific, London: Lawrence and Wishart.

Featherstone, D. (1998): Some versions of militant particularism: A review article of David Harvey's 'Justice, nature and the geography of difference', in: Antipode 30, pp. 19-25.

Featherstone, D., Ince, A. Mackinnon, D., Strauss, K. and Cumbers, A. (2012): Progressive Localism and the Construction of Political Alternatives, in: Transactions of the Institute of British Geographers 37(2), pp. 177-182.

Fickey, A. (2011): 'The Focus has to be on Helping People Make a Living': Exploring Diverse Economies and Alternative Economic Spaces, in: Geography Compass 5(5), pp. 237-248.

Fickey, A. and Hanraham, K. (forthcoming): Moving beyond Neverland: reflecting on the state of the diverse economies program and the study of alternative economic spaces, in: ACME.

Financial Services Authority (2010): Financial Returns of Credit Unions, available at: www.fsa.gov.uk/smallfirms/resources/fact-sheets/pdfs/creditunionstats_09.pdf [first accessed January 2013].

Fisher, I. (1933): Stamp Scrip, New York: Adelphi.

Freidberg, S. (2003): Cleaning up down South: Supermarkets, ethical trade and African horticulture, in: Social and Cultural Geography 4 (1), pp. 27-43.

Fuller, D. (1998): Credit Union Development: Financial Inclusion and Exclusion, in: Geoforum 29(2), pp. 145-158.

Fuller, D. and Jonas, A.E.G. (2002): Institutionalising Future Geographies of Financial Inclusion: National Legitimacy versus Local Autonomy in the British Credit Union Movement, in: Antipode 34, pp. 85-110.

Fuller, D. and Jonas, A.E.G. (2003): Alternative Financial Spaces, in: A. Leyshon, R. Lee and C. Williams (eds.), Alternative Economic Spaces, London: Sage, pp. 55-73.

Fuller, D., Jonas, A.E.G. and Lee, R. (2010a): Editorial Introduction, in: D. Fuller, A.E.G. Jonas and R. Lee (eds.), Interrogating Alterity: Alternative Economic and Political Spaces, Farnham: Ashgate, pp. xxiii-xxvii.

Fuller, D., Jonas, A.E.G. and Lee, R. (eds.) (2010b): Interrogating alterity: Alternative economic and political spaces, Farnham: Ashgate.

Gelleri, C. (2005): Assoziative Wirtschaftsräume: Regionalentwicklung mit Regiogeld, in: Fragen der Freiheit – Beiträge zur freiheitlichen Ordnung von Kultur, Staat und Wirtschaft 269.

Gertler, M.S. and Vinodrai, T. (2005): Learning from America? Knowledge Flows and Industrial Practices of German Firms in North America, in: Economic Geography 81(1), pp. 31-52.

Gesell, S. (1958): The Natural Economic Order, London: Owen.

Gibson, K., Cahill, A. and McKay, D. (2010): Rethinking the dynamics of rural transformation: performing different development pathways in a Philippine municipality, in: Transactions of the Institute of British Geographers 35(2), pp. 237-255.

Gibson-Graham, J.K. (1996): The End of Capitalism (as we knew it): A Feminist Critique of Political Economy, Minneapolis: University of Minnesota Press.

Gibson-Graham, J.K. (2002): Beyond Global vs. Local: Economic Politics Outside the Binary Frame, in: A. Herod and M. Wright (eds.), Geographies of Power: Placing Scale, Oxford: Blackwell, pp. 25-60.

Gibson-Graham, J.K. (2003): The end of Capitalism (as we knew it) – A Feminist Critique of Political Economy, Minneapolis, London: University of Minnesota Press.

Gibson-Graham, J.K. (2006): A Postcapitalist Politics, Minneapolis: University of Minnesota Press.

Gibson-Graham, J.K. (2008): Diverse Economies: Performative Practices for 'Other' Worlds, in: Progress in Human Geography 32(5), pp. 613-632.

Gibson-Graham, J.K. (2011): Forging Post-development Partnerships: Possibilities for Local and Regional Development, in A. Pike, A. Rodríguez-Pose and J. Tomaney (eds.), Handbook of Local and Regional Development, London: Routledge, pp. 226-236.

Gibson-Graham, J.K., Resnick, S. and Wolff, R. (eds.) (2001): Re/Presenting Class: Essays in Postmodern Marxism, Durham: Duke University Press.

Girod, S. (2005): The human resource management practice of retail branding: An ethnography within oxfam trading division in: International Journal of Retail & Distribution Management 33(7), pp. 514-530.

Godschalk, H. (2006): Streitfall Regionalwährungen, in: Zeitschrift für Sozialökonomie 43(149), pp. 26-28.

Goodman, D., DuPuis, E.M. and Goodman, M. (2012): Alternative food networks: Knowledge, practice and politics. London: Routledge.

Goodman, M. (2004): Reading Fair Trade: Political Ecological Imaginary and the Moral Economy of Fair Trade Foods, in: Political Geography 23, pp. 891-915.

Goodman, M. (2010): The mirror of consumption: Celebritization, developmental consumption and the shifting cultural politics of fair trade, in: Geoforum 41(1), pp. 104-116.

Goodman, M. and Barnes, C. (2011): Star/poverty space: The making of the 'development celebrity', in: Celebrity Studies 2(1), pp. 69-85.

Goss, J. (2004): Geographies of consumption I, in: Progress in Human Geography 28(3), pp. 369-380.

Gough, J. (2012): Capital Accumulation in Space, Capital-labour Relations and Political Strategy, in: A.E.G. Jonas and A. Wood (eds.), Territory, the State and Urban Politics, Farnham: Ashgate, pp. 89-112.

Gregson, N., Brooks, K. and Crewe, L. (2000): Narratives of consumption and the body in the space of the charity/shop, in: P. Jackson, M. Lowe, D. Miller and F. Mort, Commercial cultures: Economies, practices, spaces, Oxford: Berg, pp. 101-122.

Gregson, N. and Crewe, L. (2003): Second-hand cultures, Oxford: Berg.

Gregson, N., Crewe, L. and Brooks, K. (2002a): Discourse, displacement, and retail practice: Some pointers from the charity retail project, in: Environment and Planning A 34(9), pp. 1661-1683.

Gregson, N., Crewe, L. and Brooks, K. (2002b): Shopping, space, practice, in: Environment and Planning D: Society and Space 20(5), pp. 597-617.

Hale, A. (2000): What hope for 'ethical' trade in the globalised garment industry?, in: Antipode 32(4), pp. 349-356.

Hale, A. and Shaw, L. (2001): Women workers and the promise of ethical trade in the globalised garment industry: A serious beginning, in: Antipode 33(3), pp. 510-530.

Hall, P.A. and Soskice, D. (eds.) (2001): Varieties of Capitalism: The Institutional Foundations of Comparative Advantage, Oxford: Oxford University Press.

Hall, S. (1998): The toad in the garden: Thatcherism among the theorists, in: C. Nelson and L. Grossberg (eds.), Marxism and the interpretation of culture, Urbana: Univeristy of Illinois Press, pp. 35-74.

Hargrave, T.J. and Van de Ven, A.H. (2006): A Collective Action Model of Institutional Innovation, in: Organization Studies 31, pp. 864-888.

Harrison, R., Newholm, T. and Shaw, D. (eds.) (2005): The ethical consumer. London: Sage.

Harvey, D. (1982): The Limits to Capital, Oxford: Blackwell.

Harvey, D. (1992): The Condition of Postmodernity, Oxford: Blackwell.

Harvey, D. (1996): Justice, nature and the geography of difference, Cambridge, Massachusetts, Oxford: Blackwell.

Harvey, D. (2000): Spaces of hope, Berkeley: University of California Press.

Harvey, D. (2001): Spaces of capital. Towards a critical geography, London, New York: Routledge.

Harvey, D. and Hayter, T. (eds.) (1993): The factory and the city, London: Mansell.

Hawkins, R. (2012a): A new frontier in development? The use of cause-related marketing by international development organisations, in: Third World Quarterly 33(10), pp. 1783-1801.

Hawkins, R. (2012b): Shopping to save lives: Gender and environment theories meet ethical consumption, in: Geoforum 43(4), pp. 750-759.

Healy, S. (2009): Alternative Economies, in: R. Kitchin and N. Thrift (eds.), The International Encyclopedia of Human Geography, Oxford: Elsevier.

Hendrickson, C. (1996): Selling guatemala: Maya export products in us mail-order catalogues, in: D. Howes (ed.), Cross-cultural consumption: Global markets, local realities, London: Routledge, pp. 106-124.

Herrmann, M. (2005): Potentiale von Regionalgeld-Initiativen als Multiplikatoren einer nachhaltigen Entwicklung, Lüneburg: Universität Lüneburg.

Herrmann, M. (2006): Fördert Regiogeld eine nachhaltige Regionalentwicklung?, in: Zeitschrift für Sozialökonomie 43(149), pp. 12-18.

Hervieux, C. (2008): Les enjeux de l'entrepreneurship social: le cas de Cooperative Coffees, une entreprise de commerce équitable au

Nord, Collection theses et memoires 203, Montréal: Cahier de la Chaire de responsabilité sociale et de développement durable.

HEYCU (Hull and East Yorkshire Credit Union) (2010): 'You and Your Money' Members' Newsletter of HEYCU, Hull: HEYCU.

Hopkins, R. (2008): The Transition Handbook: from oil dependency to local resilience, Totnes: Green Books.

Horne, E. (1998): Charity shops in the uk, in: International Journal of Retail & Distribution Management 26(4), pp. 155-161.

Horne, E. and Broadridge, A. (1995): Charity shops: A classification by merchandise mix, in: International Journal of Retail & Distribution Management 23(7), pp. 17-23.

Hubert, E.M. (2007): Marktversagen, Verschwendung und bürgerschaftliches Engagement: Versuch zur ökonomischen Begründung von Regionalgeld, in: Zeitschrift für Sozialökonomie 44, pp. 24-28.

Hughes, A. (2000): Retailers, knowledges, and changing commodity networks: The case of the cut flower trade, in: Geoforum 31(2), pp. 175-190.

Hughes, A. (2005): Corporate strategy and the management of ethical trade: The case of the UK food and clothing retailers, in: Environment and Planning A 37(7), pp. 1145-1163.

Hughes, A., Wrigley, N. and Buttle, M. (2010): Ethical campaigning and buyer-driven commodity chains: Transforming retailers' purchasing practices?, in: M. Goodman, D. Goodman and M. Redclift (eds.), Consuming space: Placing consumption in perspective, Farnham: Ashgate, pp. 123-146.

Huybrechts, B. (2007): Fondements et implications de la diversité organisationnelle au sein du commerce équitable, in: Annals of Public and Cooperative Economics 78, pp. 195-218.

Huybrechts, B. (2012): Fair Trade Organizations and Social Enterprise. Social Innovation through Hybrid Organization Models, New York: Routledge.

Huybrechts, B. and Defourny, J. (2008): Are Fair Trade Organizations necessarily Social Enterprises?, in: Social Enterprise Journal 4, pp. 186-201.

Huybrechts, B. and Mertens, S. (2011): Renewable Energy Source Co-operatives (REScoops): Assets, Obstacles and Diffusion Strategies, 3rd International Social Innovation Research Conference, London.

Huybrechts, B. and Nicholls, A. (2012): Social entrepreneurship: defi-nitions, drivers and challenges, in: C.K. Volkmann, K.O. Tokarski and K. Ernst (eds.), Social Entrepreneurship and Social Business. An Introduction and Discussion with Case Studies, Wiesbaden: Springer Gabler, pp. 31-48.

Jackson, T. (ed.) (2006): The earthscan reader in sustainable consump-tion. London: Earthscan.

Jaffee, D. (2010): Fair Trade Standards, Corporate Participation, and Social Movement Responses in the United States, in: Journal of Business Ethics 92, pp. 267-285.

John, S. (2012): Spain barter economy wins followers in grip of crisis, in: Reuters, 20. February, available at: www.reuters.com/article/ 2012/02/20/us-spain-barter-idUSTRE81J0NJ20120220 [first ac-cessed February 2013].

Johnston, J. (2002): Consuming social justice: Fair trade shopping and alternative development, in: J. Goodman (ed.), Protest and globali-sation, Annandale: Pluto Press, pp. 38-56.

Johnston, J. (2008): The citizen-consumer hybrid: Ideological tensions and the case of whole foods market, in: Theory and Society 37(3), pp. 229-270.

Johnston, J., Biro, A. and MacKendrick, N. (2009): Lost in the super-market: The corporate-organic foodscape and the struggle for food democracy, in: Antipode 41(3), pp. 509-532.

Johnston, J. and Szabo, M. (2011): Reflexivity and the whole foods market consumer: The lived experience of shopping for change, in: Agriculture and Human Values 28(3), pp. 303-319.

Jonas, A.E.G and Wood, A. (eds.) (2012): Territory, the State and Ur-ban Politics, Farnham: Ashgate.

Jonas, A.E.G. (1996): Local Labour Control Regimes: Uneven Devel-opment and the Social Regulation of Production, in: Regional Stud-ies 30, pp. 323-338.

Jonas, A.E.G. (2006): Pro Scale: Further Reflections on the 'Scale Debate' in Human Geography, in: Transactions of the Institute of British Geographers 31, pp. 399-406.

Jonas, A.E.G. (2010): 'Alternative' This ... 'Alternative' That ... Interrogating Alterity and Diversity, in: D. Fuller, A.E.G. Jonas and R. Lee (eds.), Interrogating Alterity: Alternative Economic and Political Spaces, Farnham: Ashgate, pp. 3-29.

Jonas, A.E.G. (2013): Alternative Regionalisms, in: Progress in Human Geography, forthcoming.

Jones, R. (2012): Credit Unions Gain New Freedoms, in: The Guardian, 6. January, available at: www.theguardian.com/2012/jan/06/credit-unions-freedoms-alternative-banks [accessed January 2013].

Kelland, K. (2007): Food miles may be green, but are they fair?, available at: www.alternet.org/printable.htm?URL=/thenews/newsdesk/LO6348234.htm [first accessed March 2007].

Klein, N. (2000): No logo, New York: Picador.

Lawson, V. (2007): Geographies of care and responsibility, in: Annals of the Association of American Geographers 97(1), pp. 1-11.

Le Velly, R. (2004): Sociologie du marché. Le commerce équitable: des échanges marchands contre le marché et dans le marché, Nantes: Université de Nantes.

Lee, R. (1999): Local Money: Geographies of Autonomy and Resistance?, in: R. Martin (ed.), Money and the Space Economy, Chichester: Wiley, pp. 207-224.

Lee, R. (2002): The economic importance of geography, in: Financial Times, 30. October, p. 20.

Lee, R. (2006): The Ordinary Economy: Tangled up in Values and Geography, in: Transactions of the Institute of British Geographers 31, pp. 413-432.

Lee, R. (2010a): Economic society/Social geography, in: S.J. Smith, R. Pain, S.A. Marston and J.P. Jones (eds.), The Sage handbook of social geographies, London: Sage Publishers, pp. 205-221.

Lee, R. (2010b): Spiders, Bees or Architects? Imagination and the Radical Immanence of Alternatives/Diversity for Political Economic

Geographies, in: D. Fuller, A.E.G. Jonas and R. Lee (eds.), Interrogating Alterity: Alternative Economic and Political Spaces, Farnham: Ashgate, pp. 273-288.

Lee, R. (2011): Ordinary Economic Geographies: Can Economic Geographies be Non-economic?, in: A. Leyshon, R. Lee, L. McDowell, P. Sunley (eds.), The SAGE Handbook of Economic Geography, Los Angeles, London, New Delhi, Singapore, Washington DC: Sage, pp. 368-382.

Lee, R. (2011): Within and Outwith/Material and Political? Local Economic Development and the Spatialities of Economic Geographies, in: A. Pike, A. Rodríguez-Pose and J. Tomaney (eds.), Handbook of Local and Regional Development, London: Routledge, pp. 193-211.

Lee, R. and Leyshon, A. (2003): Conclusions: Re-making Geographies and the Construction of 'Spaces of Hope', in: A. Leyshon, R. Lee and C. Williams (eds.), Alternative Economic Spaces, London: Sage, pp. 193-198.

Lee, R., Leyshon, A., Aldridge, T., Tooke, J., Williams, C. and Thrift, N. (2004): Making Geographies and Histories? Constructing Local Circuits of Value, in: Environment and Planning D: Society and Space 22, pp. 595-617.

Levy, D. and Scully, M. (2007): The Institutional Entrepreneur as Modern Prince: The Strategic Face of Power in Contested Fields, in: Organization Studies 28, pp. 971-991.

Lewis, T. and Potter, E. (eds.) (2011): Ethical consumption: A critical introduction, London: Routledge.

Leyshon, A. (2005): Introduction: Diverse economies, Antipode 37(5), pp. 856-862.

Leyshon, A., Lee, R. and Williams, C. (eds.) (2003): Alternative Economic Spaces, London: Sage.

Leyshon, A., Lee, R., Sunley, P. and McDowell, L. (2011): Introduction, in: A. Leyshon, R. Lee, P. Sunley and L. McDowell (eds.), The Sage Handbook of Economic Geography, London: Sage, pp. 1-20.

Leyshon, A. and Thrift, N. (1997): Money/Space: Geographies of Monetary Transformation, London: Routledge.

Lincoln, A. (2003): Alternative Work Spaces, in: A. Leyshon, R. Lee and C. Williams (eds.), Alternative Economic Spaces, London: Sage, pp. 107-128.

Lionais, D. (2010): Social Enterprise and Socio-legal Structure: Constructing Alternative Institutional Spaces for Economic Development, in: D. Fuller, A.E.G. Jonas and R. Lee (eds.), Interrogating Alterity: Alternative Economic and Political Spaces, Farnham: Ashgate, pp. 223-240.

Littler, J. (2009): Radical consumption, Maidenhead: Open University Press.

Littrell, M. and Dickson, M. (1999): Social responsibility in the global market: Fair trade of cultural products, Thousand Oaks: Sage.

Lloyd, T. (1994): The charity business: The new philanthropists, London: John Murray.

Loorbach, D. (2007): Transition Management. New Mode of Governance for Sustainable Development, Utrecht: International Books.

Low, W. and Davenport, E. (2005): Postcards from the edge: Maintaining the 'alternative' character of fair trade, in: Sustainable Development 13(3), pp. 143-153.

Lowe, M. (2002): Commentary – taking economic and cultural geographies seriously, in: Tijdschrift voor Economische en Sociale Geografie 93(1), pp. 5-7.

Lyon, S. (2006): Evaluating fair trade consumption: Politics, defetishization and producer participation, in: International Journal of Consumer Studies 30(5), pp. 452-464.

Macgregor, J. and Vorley, B. (2006): Fair miles? The concept of 'food miles' through a sustainable development lens, in: International Institute for Environment and Development (IIED), available at: www.iied.org/SM/index.html [first accessed March 2007].

Mackintosh, M. and Wainwright, H. (eds.) (1987): A Taste of Power: the Politics of Local Economics, London: Verso.

Maguire, S., Hardy, C. and Lawrance, T.B. (2004): Institutional Entrepreneurship in Emerging Fields: HIV/AIDS Treatment Advocacy in Canada, in: Academy of Management Journal 47, pp. 657-679.

Mair, J. and Marti, I. (2006): Social entrepreneurship research: A source of explanation, prediction, and delight, in: Journal of World Business 41, pp. 36-44.

Malpass, A., Cloke, P., Barnett, C. and Clarke, D. (2007): Fair trade urbanism?: The politics of place beyond place in the bristol fairtrade city campaign, in: International Journal of Urban and Regional Research 31(3), pp. 633-645.

Mangan, L. (2011): Happy Christmas? Happy Craft Fair!, in: The Guardian Weekend, 10. December.

Marston, S.A., Jones III, J.P. and Woodward, K. (2005): Human Geography without Scale, in: Transactions of the Institute of British Geographers 30(4), pp. 416-432.

Marx, K. (1976): Ökonomische Manuskripte 1857-58 (Grundrisse), Berlin: Dietz Verlag.

Marx, K. (1977): Capital, Vol. 1, New York: Random House.

Massey, D. (2004): Geographies of responsibility, in: Geografiska Annaler 86(1), pp. 5-18.

Maurer, B. (2003): Uncanny exchange: the posibilities and failures of 'making change' with alternative money forms, in: Environment and Planning D: Society and Space 21(3), pp. 317-340.

McArthur, A., McGregor, A. and Stewart, R. (1993): Credit Unions and Low-income Communities, in: Urban Studies 30(2), pp. 399-416.

McCarthy, J. (2006): Rural geography: alternative rural economies – the search for alterity in forests, fisheries, food, and fair trade, in: Progress in Human Geography 30(6), pp. 803-811.

McKinnon, K. (2010): Diverse Present(s), Alternative Futures, in: D. Fuller, A.E.G. Jonas and R. Lee (eds.), Interrogating Alterity: Alternative Economic and Political Spaces, Farnham: Ashgate, pp. 259-272.

Meritt, R. (2010): How Alternative are Alternative Economic Spaces? A Study of Credit Unions in Hull, unpublished undergraduate dissertation, Department of Geography, University of Hull (available by request from the Brynmor Jones Library, University of Hull).

Meßenzehl, D. (2006): Der Chiemgauer – Ein Instrument der Regionalentwicklung mit Zukunft? Erstellung eines Stimmungsbildes der Regionalwährung aus Sicht der Bevölkerung, Diplomarbeit an der Fakultät für Geowissenschaften, Geographie und Astronomie der Universität Wien, available at: www.chiemgauer.info/fileadmin/user_upload/Theorie/DiplomarbeitUniWienMessenzehl.pdf [first accessed November 2012]

Micheletti, M. (2003): Shopping as political activity, in: Axess (9).

Miller, D. (2001): The poverty of morality, in: Journal of Consumer Culture 1(2), pp. 225-243.

Mingione, E. (1991): Fragmented Societies. A Sociology of Economic Life beyond the Market Paradigm, Oxford: Basil Blackwell.

Mirror (2012): Greedy banks beware: Credit Unions are fairer alternative, 11. January, available at www.mirror.co.uk/money/personal-finance/greedy-banks-beware-credit-unions-157988 [first accessed January 2012]

Moore, G. (2004): The Fair Trade movement: parameters, issues and future research, in: Journal of Business Ethics 53, 73-86.

Moore, G., Gibbon, J. and Slack, R. (2006): The mainstreaming of Fair Trade: a macromarketing perspective, in: Journal of Strategic Marketing 14, pp. 329-352.

Moore, G., Slack, R. and Gibbon, J. (2009): Criteria for Responsible Business Practice in SMEs: An Exploratory Case of U.K. Fair Trade Organisations, in: Journal of Business Ethics 89, pp. 173-188.

Morgan, K., Marsden, T. and Murdoch, J. (2006): Worlds of food: Place, power, and provenance in the food chain, Oxford: Oxford University Press.

Mulgan, G., Tucker, S., Ali, R. and Sanders, B. (2007): Social innovation: what it is, why it matters and how it can be accelerated, Working Paper, Oxford: Skoll Centre for Social Entrepreneurship.

Mulligan, C. (2007): Geographies of voluntarism: Mapping the terrain, in: Geography Compass 1(2), pp. 183-199.

Mundell, R. (1961): A Theory of Optimum Currency Areas, in: American Economic Review 51(4), pp. 657-665.

Münkner, H.-H. (2004): Multi-stakeholder co-operatives and their legal framework, in: C. Borzaga and R. Spear (eds.), Trends and challenges for Co-operatives and Social Enterprises in developed and transition countries, Trento: Edizioni 31, pp. 49-82.

Mutersbaugh, T. (2002): The number is the beast: A political economy of organic-coffee certification and producer unionism, in: Environment and Planning A 34(7), pp. 1165-1184.

NACUW (National Association of Credit Union Workers) (1999): Response to Her Majesty's Treasury's Consultation Document, Proposed Amendments to the Credit Unions Act 1979, NACUW: Unpublished mimeo.

NEF (New Economics Foundation) (2010): Re-imagining the High Street: Escape from Clone Town Britain, London: New Economics Foundation.

NEWS (2007): Professionalisation, available at: www.worldshops.org/worldshops/professionalisation.html [first accessed October 2007].

Nicholls, A. (2002): Strategic options in fair trade retailing, in: International Journal of Retail & Distribution Management 30, pp. 6-17.

Nicholls, A. (ed.) (2006): Social Entrepreneurship. New Models of Sustainable Social Change, Oxford: Oxford University Press.

Nicholls, A. and Murdock, A. (2012): Social Innovation: Blurring Boundaries to Reconfigure Markets, New York: Palgrave Macmillan.

Nicholls, A. and Opal, C. (2005): Fair Trade. Market-driven Ethical Consumption, London: Sage Publications.

Norberg-Hodge, H. and Mayo, E. (1996): Foreword, in: R. Douthwaite (ed.), Short Circuit: Strengthening Local Economies for Security in an Uncertain World, Totnes, Devon: Green Books, pp. 1-3.

North, P. (2002): LETS in a cold climate: Green Dollars, self help and neo-liberal welfare reform in New Zealand, in: Policy and Politics 30(4), pp. 483-500.

North, P. (2006): Constructing Civil Society? Green money in transition in Hungary, in: Review of International Political Economy 13 (1), pp. 28-52.

North, P. (2007): Money and Liberation: The Micropolitics of Alternative Currency Movements, Minneapolis: University of Minnesota Press.

North, P. (2010a): Eco-localisation as a progressive response to peak oil and climate change – A sympathetic critique, in: Geoforum 41 (4), pp. 585-594.

North, P. (2010b): Local Money, Dartington: Green Books.

Nyssens, M. (ed.) (2006): Social Enterprise. At the crossroads of market, public policies and civil society, London: Routledge.

Oxfam (2007a): Clothing, available at: www.oxfam.org.uk/shop/ highstreet/clothing.htm [first accessed December 2007].

Oxfam (2007b): Oxfam's ethical purchasing policy, available at: www.oxfam.org.uk/shop/fairtrade.htm [first accessed December 2007].

Paech, N. (2008): Regionalwährungen als Bausteine einer Postwachstumsökonomie, in: Zeitschrift für Sozialökonomie 45(158/ 159), pp. 10-19.

Parsons, E. (2002): Charity retail: Past, present and future, in: International Journal of Retail & Distribution Management 30(12), pp. 586-594.

Parsons, E. (2004a): Charity shop managers in the uk: Becoming more professional?, in: Journal of Retailing and Consumer Services 11(5), pp. 259-268.

Parsons, E. (2004b): Charity retailing in the uk: A typology, in: Journal of Retailing and Consumer Services 11(1), pp. 31-40.

Parsons, E. (2006): The voluntary spaces of charity shops: Workplaces or domestic spaces?, in: D. Conradson and C. Milligan (eds.), Landscapes of voluntarism, Bristol: The Policy Press, pp. 231-247.

Parsons, E. and Broadridge, A. (2004): Managing change in nonprofit organizations: The uk charity retail sector, in: Voluntas: International Journal of Voluntary and Nonprofit Organizations 15(3), pp. 227-242.

Peck, J. and Theodore, N. (2007): Variegated Capitalism, in: Progress in Human Geography 31, pp.731-772.

Petrella, F. (2003): Une analyse néo-institutionnaliste des structures de propriété 'multi-stakeholder'. Une application aux organisations de développement local, thèse en vue de l'obtention du grade de docteur en sciences économiques, Louvain: Université Catholique de Louvain.

Phills, J.A.J., Deiglmeier, K. and Miller, D.T. (2008): Rediscovering Social Innovation, in: Stanford Social Innovation Review Fall 2008, pp. 34-43.

Princen, T., Maniates, M. and Conca, K. (eds.) (2002): Confronting consumption, Cambridge, MA: MIT Press.

Rangneker, D. and Wilkinson, J. (2011): (New) borders of consumption, in: Environment and Planning A 43(9), pp. 2007-2011.

Raynolds, L.T. and Long, M.A. (2007): Fair/Alternative Trade: historical and empirical dimensions, in: L.T. Raynolds, D.L. Murray and J. Wilkinson (eds.), Fair Trade. The Challenges of Transforming Globalization, London: Routledge, pp. 15-32.

Raynolds, L.T. and Wilkinson, J. (2007): Fair Trade in the agriculture and food sector, in: L.T. Raynolds, D.L. Murray and J. Wilkinson (eds.), Fair Trade. The Challenges of Transforming Globalization, London: Routledge, pp. 33-48.

Raynolds, L.T., Murray, D.L. and Wilkinson, J. (eds.) (2007): Fair Trade. The challenges of transforming globalization, London, Routledge.

Redclift, M. (1997): Wasted: Counting the costs of global consumption, London: Earthscan.

Reed, D. (2009): What do Corporations have to do with Fair Trade? Positive and Normative Analysis from a Value Chain Perspective, in: Journal of Business Ethics 86, pp. 3-26.

REScoop.EU (2011): Fostering citizen involvement to reach the EU 20-20 goals, Brussels: Federation of citizen groups and associations for renewable energy.

Roozen, N. and Van der Hoff Boersma, F. (2001): L'aventure du commerce équitable. Une alternative à la mondialisation, Paris: JC Lattès.

Rösl, G. (2005): Regionalwährungen in Deutschland, in: Zeitschrift für Wirtschaftspolitik 85(3), pp. 182-190.

Rösl, G. (2006a): Komplementärwährungen in Deutschland, Frankfurt: Deutsche Bundesbank.

Rösl, G. (2006b): Regionalwährungen in Deutschland – Lokale Konkurrenz für den Euro? Frankfurt: Deutsche Bundesbank.

Rossi, U. (2012): On the varying ontologies of capitalism: Embeddedness, dispossession, subsumption, in: Progress in Human Geography 37(3), pp. 731-772.

Routledge, P. (1997): Imagineering of resistance: Pollok free state and the practice of postmodern politics, in: Transactions of the Institute of British Geographers 22(3), pp. 359-376.

Routledge, P. (2003): Convergence space: process geographies of grassroots globalization networks, in: Transactions of the Institute of British Geographers 28, pp. 333-349.

Royte, E. (2005): Garbage land: On the secret trail of trash, New York: Back Bay Books.

Samers, M. (2005): The myopia of 'diverse economies', or a critique of the 'informal economy', in: Antipode 37(5), pp. 875-886.

Samers, M. and Pollard, J. (2010): Alterity's Geographies: Socio-territoriality and Difference in Islamic Banking and Finance, in: D. Fuller, A.E.G. Jonas, R. Lee (eds.), Interrogating Alterity: Alternative Economic and Political Spaces, Farnham: Ashgate, pp. 47-58.

Santos, F.M. (2012): A Positive Theory of Social Entrepreneurship, in: Journal of Business Ethics 111(3), pp. 335-351.

Sassatelli, R. (2006): Virtue, responsibility and consumer choice: Framing critical consumerism, in: J. Brewer and F. Trentmann (eds.), Consuming cultures, global perspectives: Historical trajectories, transnational exchanges, London: Berg, pp. 219-250.

Sayer, A. and Storper, M. (1997): Ethics unbound: For a normative turn in social theory, in: Environment and Planning D: Society and Space 15(1), pp. 1-17.

Schreven, S., Spoelstra, S. and Svensson, P. (2008): Alternatively, in: Ephemera 8(2), pp. 129-136.

Schroeder, R. (2006): Community Exchange and Trading Systems in Germany, in: International Journal of Complementary Currency Research 10, pp. 24-42.

Scott Cato, M. (2006): How the euro threatens the well-being of the planet and its people, in: M. Baimbridge, B. Birkitt and P. Whyman (eds.), Implications of the Euro: a critical perspective from the left, London: Routledge, pp. 157-167.

Selfa, T. and Qazi, J. (2005): Place, Taste, or Face-to-Face? Understanding Producer-Consumer Networks in "Local" Food Systems in Washington State, in: Agriculture and Human Values 22(4), pp. 451-464.

Seyfang, G. (2006a): Ecological citizenship and sustainable consumption: Examining local organic food networks, in: Journal of Rural Studies 22(4), pp. 383-395.

Seyfang, G. (2006b): Sustainable Consumption, the New Economics and Community Currencies: Developing New Institutions for Environmental Governance, in: Regional Studies 40(7), pp. 781-791.

Seyfang, G. (2010): Time Banking: A New Economics Alternative, in: D. Fuller, A.E.G. Jonas and R. Lee (eds.), Interrogating Alterity: Alternative Economic and Political Spaces, Farnham: Ashgate, pp. 193-206.

Shuman, M. (2001): Going Local: Creating Self Reliant Communities in a Global Age, London: Routledge.

Simms, A. (2007): Tescopoly, London: Constable.

Smith, D. (2000): Moral geographies: Ethics in a world of difference, Edinburgh: Edinburgh University Press.

Smith, S. (2005): States, markets and an ethic of care, in: Political Geography 24, pp. 1-20.

Spehl, H. (2008): Welchen Beitrag zur Regionalentwicklung können Regionalgelder leisten?, in: Zeitschrift für Sozialökonomie 46(185/186), pp. 20-25.

Stiglitz, D.J. (2009): Moving beyond market fundamentalism to a more balanced economy, in: Annals of Public & Cooperative Economics 80, pp. 345-360.

Studzinski, J. (2013): Germany is right: there is no right to profit, but the right to work is essential, in: The Guardian, 6. February, available at: www.guardian.co.uk/commentisfree/2013/feb/06/germany-success-humanity-medium-firms [first accessed February 2013].

Thiel, C. (2011): Complementary Currencies in Germany: the Regiogeld system, in: International Journal of Community Currency Research 15, pp. 17-21.

Tracey, P., Phillips, N. and Jarvis, O. (2011): Bridging Institutional Entrepreneurship and the Creation of New Organizational Forms: A Multilevel Model, in: Organization Science 22, pp. 60-80.

Van der Hoff Boersma, F. (2009): The Urgency and Necessity of a Different Type of Market: The Perspective of Producers Organized Within the Fair Trade Market, in: Journal of Business Ethics 86, pp. 51-61.

Volkmann, K. (2009): Regional – und trotzdem global: Solidarische Ökonomie im Spannungsfeld zwischen Regionalität und Globalität. Eine explorative Studie zu Regionalwährungen, Münster: Lit Verlag.

Von Osten, M. (2010): Editorial – 'In Search of the postcapitalist self', in: e-flux journal 17, available at: www.e-flux.com/journal/editorial%E2%80%94%E2%80%9Cin-search-of-the-postcapitalist-self%E2%80%9D/ [first accessed December 2012].

Vural, M. (2008): Consuming the campesino, in: Cultural Studies 22 (5), pp. 654-679.

Ward, K. and Jonas, A.E.G. (2004): Competitive City Regionalism as a Politics of Space: A Critical Reinterpretation of the 'New Regionalism', in: Environment and Planning A 36(12), pp. 2119-2139.

WFTO (World Fair Trade Organization) (2013): Code of practice, available at: www.wfto.com/index.php?option=com_content&task=view&id=39&Itemid=125 [first accessed February 2013].

Williams, C., Aldridge, T., Lee, R., Leyshon, A., Thrift, N. and Tooke, J. (2001): Bridges into work? An Evaluation of Local Exchange Trading Schemes (LETS), Bristol: The Policy Press.

Williams, C., Aldridge, T. and Tooke, J. (2003): Alternative Exchange Spaces, in A. Leyshon, R. Lee and C. Williams (eds.), Alternative Economic Spaces, London: Sage, pp. 151-167.

Williams, C., Nadin, S., Rodgers, P. and Round, J. (2012): Rethinking the Nature of Community Economies, in: Community Development Journal 47(2), pp. 216-231.

Williams, R. (1989): Resources of hope, London: Verso.

Wilson, B. (2010): Indebted to Fair Trade? Coffee and crisis in Nicaragua, in: Geoforum 41(1), pp. 84-92.

Wittel, A. (2001): Toward a network sociality, in: Theory, Culture & Society 18(6), pp. 51-76.

WOCCU (World Council of Credit Unions) (2004): 2004 Statistical Report, available at: www.woccu.org/index [first accessed September 2005].

Woodin, M. and Lucas, C. (2004): Green Alternatives to Globalisation: a Manifesto, London: Pluto.

Wright, C. (2004): Consuming lives, consuming landscapes: interpreting advertisements for cafédirect coffees, in: Journal of International Development 16(5), pp. 665-680.

Young, I.M. (1990): Justice and the politics of difference, Princeton: Princeton University Press.

Notes on Contributors

Raymond Bryant is Professor of Political Ecology at King's College, London. His main areas of research include political geography, political ecology, NGOs as well as environmental policy and conflict in the Global South.

Michael K. Goodman teaches Geography as Senior Lecturer at King's College, London. His research focuses on consumption and commodity geographies, the cultural politics of alternative food networks as well as ethical and fair trade systems.

Sebastian Hillebrand lectures Geography as Research and Teaching Associate at the Catholic University of Eichstätt-Ingolstadt. He is a cultural geographer with research interests in social innovation and creative industries.

Benjamin Huybrechts teaches Management as Assistant Professor at the HEC Management School, University of Liège. His research interests include the fields of organizational diversity and social innovation, social enterprises, fair trade and renewable energy source cooperatives.

Andrew E.G. Jonas is Professor of Human Geography at the University of Hull. He is an urban political geographer with research interests in the economic governance and redevelopment of cities and regions in the USA and Europe.

Roger Lee is Professor Emeritus at the School of Geography, Queen Mary University of London. His research interests include socio-cultural relations and economic geographies, alternative economic geographies, finance and emerging markets.

Peter North is Reader in Alternative Economies in the Department of Geography and Planning at the University of Liverpool. His current research interests focus on social movements, alternative currencies, localization strategies and politics of climate change.

Katinka Weber lectures in Latin American Anthropology and Sociology as University Teacher at the University of Liverpool. Her research interests are in the fields of development studies and the state, social change and resistance studies as well as governance studies and citizenship.

Hans-Martin Zademach is Professor of Economic Geography at the Catholic University of Eichstätt-Ingolstadt. His current research focuses on transnational production networks and financial geographies with a particular focus on corporate responsibility and sustainable economic practices.